SIRSHREE

Author of the bestseller *The Source...Power Of Happy Thoughts* published in several languages

ULTIMATE PURPOSE OF SUCCESS

Achieving and Inspiring Others to Achieve Success in All Five Realms of Life

Ultimate Purpose of Success
By **Sirshree** Tejparkhi

Copyright © Tejgyan Global Foundation
All Rights Reserved 2012

Tejgyan Global Foundation is a charitable organization
with its headquarters in Pune, India.

ISBN : 9788184153026

Published by WOW Publishings Pvt. Ltd., India

First edition published in October 2012
Fourth reprint in February 2025

Printed and bound by Trinity Academy For Corporate Training Ltd, Pune

Copyright and publishing rights are vested exclusively with WOW Publishings Pvt. Ltd. This book is sold subject to the condition that it shall not by way of trade or otherwise, be lent, resold, hired out, or otherwise circulated without the publisher's prior written consent in any form of binding or cover other than that in which it is published and without a similar condition including this condition being imposed on the subsequent purchaser and without limiting the rights under copyright reserved above, no part of this publication may be reproduced, stored in or introduced into a retrieval system, or transmitted, in any form, or by any means, electronic, mechanical, photocopying, recording or otherwise, without the prior written permission of both the copyright owner and the above-mentioned publisher of this book. Any person who does any unauthorized act in relation to this publication may be liable to criminal prosecution and civil claims for damages.

Although the author and publisher have made every effort to ensure accuracy of content in this book, they hereby disclaim any liability to any party for any loss, damage, or disruption caused by errors or omissions, resulting from negligence, accident, or any other cause. Readers are advised to take full responsibility to exercise discretion in understanding and applying the content of this book.

*This book is dedicated to
every person of the world
who is passionate about progress,
a devotee of knowledge,
a witness of Self,
and who aims to achieve
the ultimate purpose of success.*

Contents

	Preface	7
	Part I : Complete Success	**9**
1.	What is Complete Success?	11
2.	Complete Blossoming and Winning	15
3.	Seven Needs of a Human Being	20
4.	How to Attain Complete Success	24
	Part II : Success in the realm of doing	**27**
5.	Self-Expansion for Innovation	29
6.	The Habit of Completion	34
7.	Impersonal Life	37
8.	Importance of Foresight	43
9.	Living for Others Because There is No Other	46
	Part III : Success in the realm of saying	**51**
10.	Communication for Self-Expression	53
11.	Powerful Personality for Self-Expression	58
	Part IV : Success in the realm of thinking	**63**
12.	Self Elevation for Productivity	65

13.	The Habit of Self-Analysis	73
14.	Truth Thinking	79
15.	Overcoming Habit Patterns	84
16.	Conquering Fear	96
17.	Power of Viveka	101
	Part V : Success in the realm of feeling	**107**
18.	Self-Energizing for Leadership	109
19.	Live in the Present	113
20.	Power of Acceptance	117
21.	Overcoming Failure	124
22.	Cultivating Courage	131
	Part VI : Success in the realm of being	**135**
23.	Self-Experience for Leadership	137
24.	Success is Your Nature	140
25.	Become Truthful	143
26.	The Contrast Mind	146
27.	Silence	152
	Appendices	**157**
	Power of Intention	159
	About Tejgyan	187

Preface

Success — this is a word which is dear to all. However, it is interesting that the definition of success for each one of us is different. Also, we all try to achieve it in our own different ways. But what is your aim behind wanting to achieve success? And what should it be?

When you have earned all the material success that this world has to offer, it can be called Outer Success. When you have developed all your inner powers, due to which no success in the world is unattainable for you, it can be called Inner Success. When you realize your true self and your true potential, it can be called Higher Success.

When you attain all the three types of success mentioned above, it is Complete Success. Thus, Complete Success can be attained when you are successful in all the five aspects of your life—doing, saying, thinking, feeling and being.

So, achieving complete success is the final aim of human life. No, it's not. There is something more. Supposing that if complete success were a person, what would it want to achieve? What would be its ultimate purpose?

The story of complete success can be written when your actions arise from your true nature. Express the qualities of your limitless and formless self in order to share your bliss with others and inspire them to achieve complete success too. This is the ultimate purpose of complete success. And this is the ultimate purpose of your life on earth. Only when you achieve this purpose, your heart will revel in the feeling of completeness and fulfilment. This is where your constant chasing after success will end.

This book presents to you several ideas, techniques and secrets for achieving complete success as well as the ultimate purpose of success. You can definitely achieve them because you are programmed for success. Looking at so many tools laid out before you, your mind may start making excuses. Here's a little secret that you can tell your mind: 'Do a little, but do it today.' Be courageous and start implementing the techniques, one by one if you may, but begin today. Start watching your feelings, thoughts, words, actions, habits and demerits, as a witness. Put a full stop to your negative thoughts. Do a little, but do it today.

If a rock needs one hundred blows of a hammer to break, it does not mean that only the hundredth blow did the job. The first blow was as important as the last one. Someone who abandons a job seeing no results in his first attempt does not know the law of consistency. Consistency is the key to success. The one who exercises every day or at least thrice a week gains the reward of good health. The student who studies every day, even for a small period of time, is the one who shines through in all his exams. The individual who works diligently every day earns prosperity. An artist who practises his art for some time every day creates a masterpiece. The seeker who has the habit of contemplating every day succeeds in understanding all the secrets of life. Thus, if you want to achieve success, put consistency into your actions. Choose the right actions, thoughts and qualities. Write them in a diary and work on them every day little by little, starting today.

Contemplate over all the points that you understood and liked in this book, and put them into action. And if you haven't liked some, or found them illogical, park them aside for the time being in one corner of your mind, just as you park your car when not in use. Don't reject them straightaway. A time will surely come when you shall understand them and put them into use as well.

To culminate your quest for success, become capable with the help of this book. The moment you become capable, success will walk up to your doorstep on its own. So, let's begin with joy the glorious journey of attaining Complete Success as well as the Ultimate Purpose of Success.

Part I

Complete Success

Blossoming, Winning and Fulfilment

1
What is Complete Success?

We all yearn for success. So, what is its definition? There are two ways success is usually looked at:

Success as per your own understanding: Self-doctrine

This kind of success is that in which you achieve what you have determined to. Here you give importance to your own opinion about success. The definition of Success here is: *You decide, you do.* In other words, when you decide upon a task and you complete it, then you are successful. You take a decision to be a carpenter. You begin to learn the art and you finally become a carpenter. Then it can be said that you have attained success. Some people might not agree that you have achieved success. They will tell you that you should have rather become a doctor or an engineer. This is what they had decided for you and hence they won't be happy with you. But if you are able to achieve what you have decided for yourself, you are successful.

Success as per what others think: Social dogma

The second kind of success is when you achieve everything which according to people is 'success'. Here you give more importance to people's views about success.

As per the societal dogma, man believes that success means having a big house, plush office, high-flying job and rich friends, without which life is a failure.

This belief of success stems from man's tendency to give importance to others' opinion, as he is a social being. He wants to be successful from people's point of view, because he longs for praise and appreciation from them. And the things that he sees all around—luxurious bungalows and cars, designations and titles at the workplace—only reinforce the wrong notion of success that he has built for himself. Man has the tendency of imitating. What he sees is what he wants. Thus everyone goes behind this pied piper of success.

An individual experiences the feelings of misery, failure, insult, fame, respect, progress, etc. in accordance to the social norms of success. Many suicides too are a direct fallout of such social dogma. A student who kills himself because of failing in examinations does so out of this false belief about success. He had gathered the wrong definition of success by listening to the world around him. He had believed this definition of success and failure. If only he was given the right guidance at the right time, he wouldn't have made such an unfortunate mistake of ending his life.

Man tends to believe others' version of success. He feels successful only when others pat him on the back and say, 'You are a success.' But success is actually *doing and accomplishing that which you decided*.

Complete Success

The question therefore is: Is success just these two points of view mentioned above? Reflect whether wanting to be successful is wanting to be *complete* and *fulfilled*? Are you complete when you have lots of money, a house, a job, status, power and talent? If your answer is yes, then ask those who have all these things. Do they consider themselves to be complete? A majority will answer in the negative. People wish to experience completeness but they have no idea of what it is.

> *When you leave your home for a few days, you make sure to meet every member of the family before leaving. If you are unable to meet even one of them, you feel a sense of incompleteness. At the railway station, right till the last moment before your train leaves, you keep thinking of that person. 'He did not come... I couldn't meet him...' You can't stop thinking about him even where you have gone. This is because you could not complete with him.*

Similarly, even if there is the slightest feeling of incompletion, then it is not complete success. Many people decide something and they do it as well. But still there is a sense of incompletion in terms of so many other things to do. So, what then is complete success? When is it is that you get rid of the feeling of incompletion?

There are also some people who are apparently successful, but have not attained complete success. They have attained outer success, some have attained inner success as well, while some have even attained higher success. When you attain all three, that is when you have achieved complete success.

When everything in life is hunky-dory and as per the wishes of our mind, we do not realize that we are content with false success, which is transient. When difficulties and sorrow enter our life, when we get dejected and feel scared, we then realize that we are not yet successful. Complete Success is a state in which your mind remains unshaken, loving, pure, obedient and integrated, in all sorts of circumstances and in the face of any difficulty. Complete success is when your body-mind is completely trained and disciplined; and it can do anything you wish to without any interference from your habits or tendencies. Complete success is when you have realized your true self and attained your highest potential.

Learn to write the story of your complete success expending the least possible energy. Use the rest of your energy to share your joy and to help others attain complete success too. This is why you have come to this world. This is the success that God wants you to achieve. This is what will give you complete satisfaction and fulfilment.

❖❖❖

Practical Exercise

Contemplate on what success is for you and which type of success do you wish to achieve.

What next?

Once you complete the exercise mentioned above, in Chapter 2 you will understand more about what complete success is all about and its relationship with winning.

2
Complete Blossoming and Winning

Complete Blossoming

How does one attain complete success? Actually, by doing nothing. Complete success is natural. You attain it by allowing yourself to unfold naturally. When all the buds in the garden fully blossom into flowers, they celebrate the glory of success. When you attain success in all the five realms—doing, saying, thinking, feeling and being—it means you have blossomed completely. Every child in this world can grow up and celebrate the glory of complete success... if only he is not hampered in the process of opening up and blossoming. Every child automatically progresses towards complete success by experimenting in all these five realms from the time he wakes up till the time he drops off to sleep. Children keep performing some experiments. They will sometimes climb atop a chair and jump down, and sometimes they will break open their toys to see what's inside. If you ask them, 'Why are you doing this?', they are amazed at your question. They think, and sometimes even tell you, 'Why shouldn't I?'

> *A child asks his father, 'I want to play drums; will you get me a set?' His father replies, 'No. If I get you drums, you will play them loud all day and disturb us.' The child earnestly says, 'No, dad! I will not disturb anyone at all. I'll play them only after everyone has gone to sleep.'*

However, these experiments stop once the child grows up. This happens because his elders and the people around him train him according to their own distorted understanding about life. The child was on the natural course of opening up and blossoming through his inquisitive experimenting, but he is held back.

When the baby is in the mother's womb, he is restricted. He wants to come out as early as possible so that he can open up and blossom. But does the child really open up and blossom in his life? Does he attain complete success? If an old man dies, you won't feel as sad for him as you would for a child. The reason is that you are aware of the possibilities of blossoming that the child could have explored, but couldn't. However, if you look at the matter of fact, how many people on earth do manage to completely blossom before dying? Most of them live a withdrawn, inhibited life, and also die that way. People live a life ridden with fear, always apprehensive of what others might think of them.

What is the probability of a seed sprouting and flourishing? If the seed is thrown on the street, it will decay and die on the same day. If sown in rocky ground, it will sprout a little and then die, because its roots cannot go deep. What if it is sown in fertile soil but in the midst of thorny bushes? Although it will grow, it will get entangled in the thorns. Though it has got good soil, it cannot progress because of bad company. Hence for complete progress, it should be free of thorny surroundings and should get ample sunlight and water. Only then can the seed thrive to its maximum potential.

When a seed receives the right soil, essential nutrients from fertilizers, right amount of water, sunlight, shade, and also the right gardener (a right mentor or a Guru), then it grows and achieves its highest state of development. Only such a seed achieves the goal of complete success.

Complete Winning

It is not being said that winning in all areas of life is success. It is being said that allowing a natural and highest expression in all areas of life is success.

> *An amateur once challenged two chess grandmasters to play simultaneously with him. He declared: 'I will play chess with both of you at the same time and will win against at least one of you.' They agreed and the game began. The two chess boards were laid on two sides of a curtain separating them. He played with both the players concurrently. After a stretch of time, he indeed won against one of them! How did an amateur accomplish this feat? He revealed his modus operandi. He had asked the first grandmaster to make the first move and told the second one that he would be making the first move. Whatever move the first grandmaster made, he made the same move against the second grandmaster. He gave the first one the same response that the second one gave him. In this manner he played and won against one of them.*

This man made very good use of his intelligence. But the question to be asked here is: Did he gain any expertise in the game of chess? Did his confidence in playing this game rise? Was he able to open up and fully blossom after playing in this manner?

People are playing the game of life in similar fashion and are concerned only whether they are winning or losing. Though some people win, what is the method they adopted to win? Does this victory help them to grow in life, for which they were born on earth? Or is only a game of deception going on? You might have seen how people often lie when they do not succeed. When people speak, they conceal, exaggerate or twist facts. A husband tells his wife that the departing time of the train is 6 o'clock, knowing well that it is actually 6:15. He is apprehensive of missing the train if his wife takes a long time to get ready. The wife knows that her husband always does this and so she takes her own sweet time to get ready. Both husband and wife are aware of each other's deceiving ways, and hence there is unnecessary pretence and conflict in their life.

When the wife asks her husband 'Did you like the food I cooked?', he always replies in the affirmative because he knows that she would be annoyed if he speaks the truth. He develops the habit of concealing, twisting or exaggerating facts. And in this manner the game of life is being played with deceit, and the growth that is meant to occur, simply does not take place. On the outside it may seem like a person has achieved success, just like the amateur who won the game of chess, but actually he does not make any progress. To achieve progress, he needs to understand the game and delve deep into its secrets.

What are the rules and principles of this game of success and failure? If you understand the rules of this game, you can revel in eternal happiness and fulfil the purpose of your life. It is for fulfilling this purpose that you were born as a human on earth. A human being possesses certain powers which other beings do not. For example, only a human being possesses the power to think. But he uses this power for trivial gains. Such gains do not at all lead to complete success.

In childhood, while playing games, there is always somebody in the group who is ridiculed by being called a 'rookie'. If that child continues to believe that he is a rookie even after growing up, he would most certainly be living an unsuccessful life ridden with fears and anxieties. These are fears arising from childhood beliefs, which remain even after growing up. Elders too develop fear by believing those who tell them, 'You might have committed sin in your previous birth due to which you are facing failures and misery in this life.' Hence acquiring right understanding in all five realms and uncovering the process of natural blossoming is the way to achieve complete success.

❖ ❖ ❖

Practical Exercise

Contemplate: In which area of life do you feel most fulfilled? Is it in work, in a relationship, in your spiritual growth endeavour (while meditating, etc.), in your fitness pursuit (while exercising), or your artistic pursuits (painting, writing, reading, singing, etc.)?

What next?

Once you complete the exercise mentioned above, then in the next chapter you will understand about which needs you are fulfilling at present and what are the higher needs you will encounter further in your life.

3
Seven Needs of a Human Being

Necessity is the mother of invention. The greatest of inventions become possible when a need arises. Bigger the need, bigger is the possibility.

Bigger the success you want in life, bigger is the discovery that will occur inside you.

There are seven needs of a human being. As is your goal, so are your needs.

First need: Air, water and food

Man's foremost necessity is air. He will be alive as long as his breathing continues. When a baby is born, the doctor first checks whether it has started breathing or not. And when someone is on his deathbed, people present at the scene check whether he is still breathing or not. Water and food are equally important for man's survival. Air, water and food are thus the first need of life. When the first need is met with, the second one is born.

Second need: Security

Man next feels the need for personal security. He builds a house to protect himself from the elements—rain, storms, heat and cold. He earns money to secure his future. Once his second necessity is fulfilled, he feels the need for the next one. If his primary necessities are not fulfilled, he does not even think about the further ones.

Third need: Comfort and convenience

When man has a means of livelihood, a home and provision for food, he then wishes for comforts. He buys appliances like the television, refrigerator, washing machine, air-conditioner, etc. He wants his family and himself to feel comfortable. When he was finding it hard to even sustain himself, he couldn't afford to think about comforts. But after his essential needs are met with, he starts thinking about his desires.

Fourth need: Love

Once his first three requirements are fulfilled, man feels the need for love. You often find that rich and spoiled children develop addictions like drugs and alcohol because they have all the comforts and luxuries. They have everything that money can buy but they don't have love. Children whose parents are seldom at home are deprived of parental love. They crave for love and try to fill this vacuum by indulging in gambling and drinking.

When man's primary requirements are taken care of, he wishes for someone to love him. He knows that the love his so-called friends give him is not real; it is only due to their greed. He wants true love. And for that reason many relationships have been made—mother, father, brother, sister, uncle, aunt, spouse, children, etc.—from whom he desires true love.

For some people the fourth need stands at the third place, and for some the third need stands at the fourth place. When these requirements are also satisfied, he moves on to his fifth need.

Fifth need: Name and fame

Man now wishes for recognition, just like an artist who earns both name and fame when his art is recognized.

He wishes to do something that will make him famous. He wants more and more people to know him. He feels this urge because even though all his basic needs are fulfilled, there remains a vacuum in his life which feels very unpleasant. He does not feel fulfilment. His success does not feel complete and so he now runs behind name and fame. Thus, with every need that is fulfilled, man moves on to the next need.

Sixth need: Utilization of innate powers

When all the above five needs are fulfilled, man thinks of exploring the powers hidden inside him and of utilizing them to their maximum potential.

He now feels that it does not matter if he earns a name or not; what matters is unleashing the potential that he is capable of. He wants to do everything that he can. Not because somebody else is doing it, but because he wants to do it. He wishes to see what heights his self-expression can reach. It is this thinking that takes him to the next level of success. He discovers that there are many things he is capable of doing. He tries to get more trained and works on unfolding all his possibilities. Thereby he reaches up to the seventh need, where he achieves the aim of Complete Success.

Seventh need: Self-Realization

Even after the fulfilment of six of his needs, man still feels an emptiness within. He has earned a name for himself, he has a high reputation and he has also utilized his hidden powers, yet he feels incomplete. The quest for *completeness* leads to the seventh and final need—Enlightenment (or self-realization, realizing who you actually are; realizing your true essence or your original nature). Until this need is fulfilled, man is going to feel empty inside. Self-realization is higher success. If self-realization is attained after fulfilment of the earlier six needs, it is complete success.

The understanding of the Ultimate Truth was missing in the first six needs. Man does not recognize his true self while fulfilling those needs. He considers himself to be the body. Air, water and food are the needs of his body, and not that of his true self. He realizes this at the seventh step.

❖❖❖

Practical Exercise

From what you have read so far, reflect on where you stand today. Which is the necessity you are working on? Whatever level you are at present, there is nothing right or wrong about it. What is important is to check the direction you feel the pull—upwards or downwards. Are you attracted more towards the lower needs or towards the higher needs? The lower needs are: tasty food, fashionable clothes, leisure tours, movies, safety, security, comforts, luxuries, name, fame, power, false love, infatuations, etc. The higher needs are—Bright love (beyond the polarities of love and hatred, it is unconditional, unquestioning, unlimited, unchanging, eternal, true love for one and all), self-realization, liberation, Bright knowledge (knowledge of the Ultimate Truth), Bright happiness (causeless and eternal inner bliss which is beyond the polarities of happiness and unhappiness), complete success, etc. Ask yourself: Are you ready for complete success?

What next?

Don't be under the wrong impression that once you attain complete success, you should abstain from delicious food, trendy clothes, travelling or using household appliances, comforts and luxuries. On the fulfilment of the seven needs and attaining complete success, every action of yours happens for the larger benefit of people. You eat, drink, sit, walk, sleep, wake up, travel, read, write... everything for the welfare of others. Your life no longer remains a 'personal' one, it becomes 'impersonal'. In other words, you begin to fulfil the ultimate purpose of success. An impersonal life is a successful life, a complete life. So, in Chapter 4, let us understand how to attain complete success.

4
How to Attain Complete Success

Complete success is attained when you succeed in all aspects of a human being. So, what is a human being after all? A human being consists of the following:

- The realm of being (consciousness)
- The realm of feeling (emotions)
- The realm of thinking (thoughts)
- The realm of saying (words)
- The realm of doing (actions)

Many a time success is understood only as being successful in the realm of actions. But what if someone has a lot of money but extremely poor relationships? Or worse, if he is constantly depressed? Or indulges in many vices? What if he is not in touch with his inner self? Is his success really success? This is why the idea of Complete Success has been brought up, which means success in all the realms of a human being.

Out of the five domains mentioned above, the core is *being*. This core, this realm of consciousness, is the missing link in most human endeavours. When you experientially know the answer to 'Who am I?' and always express from that premise—only then your success is truly complete. This is the seventh need of self-realization as seen in the previous chapter.

You can progress naturally towards success by examining each of the realms and unleashing the process of natural blossoming. This is done through the Complete Success System which is as follows:

- Uncover the Natural Self within you in the realm of Being (consciousness)

- Unlock the Natural Leader within you in the realm of Feeling (emotions)

- Unravel the Natural Achiever within you in the realm of Thinking (thoughts)

- Untie the Natural Communicator within you in the realm of Saying (words)

- Unleash the Natural Innovator within you in the realm of Doing (actions)

❖❖❖

Practical Exercise

Contemplate as to which aspect of yours is strong and which is weak.

What next?

Uncover! Unlock! Unravel! Untie! Unleash! For these five steps of the Complete Success System, keenly read and follow each of the five parts described in the ensuing pages. We shall begin from success in the realm of doing and move step by step to success to the realm of being. Let's begin with 'Unleashing the Natural Innovator within you' in Part II.

Part II

Success in the realm of doing

Unleash the Natural Innovator within you

5
Self-Expansion for Innovation

Innovation is the ability to think new ideas and execute them successfully. So, it is not just thinking. It is completing. That is why it is in the realm of doing. What is required for innovation is the virtue of creativity and the habit of completion. There are people who work for years together on improving their creativity or training themselves in execution and completion and getting out of procrastination. However, they usually fail since it is not a natural self-expansion, but more of an act of will. There is something that should happen for allowing innovation to occur naturally... and that is having a vision. A lot of businessmen who have started their own companies after having left their jobs find that suddenly they are compelled to be creative and to complete what they intend to create. Employees who have taken on a vision automatically become innovative. Mothers who have a vision for their children automatically turn resourceful. What is it that naturally propels them to do that? It is an endearing vision. Having a personal vision helps you attain higher realms of innovation. But if your vision is impersonal, then your highest possibility begins to unfold.

The virtue of creativity

A simple secret of success is:

See what everyone is seeing, but think what no one else is thinking.

If you can't think creatively, be in the company of those who can.

An excellent way to achieve success is to bring about an improvement (innovation) in whatever you do—your work, the goods you sell, the selfless services that you render, the words you speak, your relationships, everything. Make them better and better. The urge to do things better is a sign of success. Along with your actions, you too keep on getting better. If you deteriorate instead, then all your actions and your job bring you false success and leave you discontented.

A developed person knows that every task he does can be done better. The secret of success lies in performing the task at hand to the best of one's ability. This belief in itself works wonders in his life.

An unsuccessful, undeveloped person carries out every task in the same old manner that he has been doing since many years. All that Mr. Unsuccessful learns is to find lame excuses for his failures. He doesn't learn to do a better job. Excuses drift him off into the lake of lethargy. Hence beware of excuses drifting you away; learn to swim by improving yourself.

Mr. Successful, on the other hand, gives regular exercise to his thinking abilities in order to hone and sharpen them. He gives his brain a dose of creative thinking ever so often. A human being uses only a small percentage of his brain power. To bring out the best that the brain can offer, it is necessary to exercise it with creative thinking. To think of ways to do things better and more creatively, you need to identify your hidden false beliefs. A simple example will illustrate what these beliefs are like. When you look at a doughnut, what can be your false beliefs about it? The first one could be that a doughnut ought to be ring-shaped.

The second one could be that it should be wheat-coloured. If you cast away these beliefs and prepare triangular, indigo-coloured doughnuts, it will be a completely new experience for the people seeing them or eating them. In this way, to practise creativity and innovation, you need to bring to light all your beliefs and preconceived notions from every aspect of your life. If you are able to break free from these beliefs and create something new, success will be at your feet. Creative thinking is food for the brain. On consuming this food, you can easily churn out new creations.

Mr. Unsuccessful keeps picking out unpleasant experiences from his memory bank and causes misery to himself. He allows unpleasant thoughts to enter and steal away his remaining level of consciousness, awareness and happiness. A successful person withdraws only creative and inspiring memories from his memory bank. He recalls beautiful and practical images and discovers new things. This quality of Mr. Successful never allows him to get bored. On the strength of this virtue, he achieves his goal of complete success laughing and playing. He always remains in touch with his higher consciousness.

◆◆◆

Practical Exercise

Examine your beliefs about success and creativity. Tick which ones from those mentioned below are true for you:

1. *I am not creative.*
2. *Creativity is an inborn skill.*
3. *Only artistic people need to be creative.*
4. *Without knowledge, I cannot be successful.*
5. *Without education, I cannot be successful.*
6. *Without English language skills, I cannot be successful.*
7. *Without luck, I cannot be successful.*
8. *Without good references and contacts, I cannot be successful.*

9. Without a woman behind me, I cannot be successful.
10. You need to be born into a wealthy family to be successful.
11. I need to know the business to become successful.
12. I need capital to become successful. So everything boils down to money.
13. Only if I have something very unique and innovative can I be successful.
14. It takes a lot of time to be successful.
15. Success comes only with experience.
16. Success means a lot of work.
17. I won't have time to sleep soundly when I become successful.
18. I need to make a lot of sacrifices to become successful.
19. I need to compromise with my personal life to become successful.
20. I will have to give up my principles and stop being honest in order to achieve success.
21. I will have more enemies than friends if I become successful.
22. I cannot be successful always. People go up the ladder but have to come down eventually.

What next?

Understand that all of the above are myths. If any of these still continue to be true for you, drop them with understanding.

For points 1 — 13, understand that though each of the given factors could be helpful in attaining success, they are not a must. Creativity can be easily attained. Innovation is already within you. And the other factors you see in the list such as money or knowledge or contacts are all helpful, but not a necessity for success. There are many real-life examples of those who did not have the money or the knowledge and yet made it to the top.

For points 14 − 16, understand that people have become successful through innovation fairly quickly and easily. People have become successful irrespective of age. If others can do it, so can you. Opportunity knocks at your door in various guises. But many people are not even aware of this and let opportunities pass. Every problem and every difficulty is an opportunity disguised in the garb of unhappiness. Most of the times, opportunity knocks at the back door, and more often than not is allowed to pass by. Be aware of every opportunity that appears in your life.

For points 17 − 23, understand that it is possible to be successful while being honest. In fact, it can be said that honesty is an essential ingredient for success. Secondly, it is possible to attain success while maintaining a healthy work-life balance. As many individuals and companies have demonstrated, it is also possible to have consistent success.

If all of these are myths and if there is one habit one needs to develop for attaining success, it would be the habit of completion. That is what we shall see in Chapter 6.

6
The Habit of Completion

The key habit for attaining success is to finish all your incomplete work on time. A successful man is one who does not fear hard work and does all that he can to complete the job, and that too on time. His understanding tells him that only those activities which are complete lead to success in this world. Half done tasks are as good as not done. Hard work and diligence are duty as well as exercise for every one of us.

The motto of the one who is a foe of hard work and a friend of food is 'give work a rest'. He can never succeed. Unsuccessful people like to believe that hard work is injurious to health. Only when the Damocles' sword hovers perilously above their head do they move and do something. Nobody dies of excessive work. Most people die from the poison of lethargy, suspicion and hatred.

You can achieve success only when you get rid of laziness. Success first demands that you take responsibility of your work, commit to it and accomplish it.

Commitment means honouring your word which you give to yourself and to others. You need to fulfil your promises. To keep a promise, you have to complete the assigned work as scheduled. You need to be courageous and use both your head and heart. As soon as you become committed, your attitude towards work becomes positive. With a positive attitude, your work is easily accomplished.

If you are not being able to finish a task, think of what is the minimum that you can do to complete it. Bear in mind that you should not allow any feelings of guilt to creep in; else you will only harm yourself. You should consider all the alternatives in such situations. You can seek advice from your colleagues for thinking up the alternatives.

Having decided to take up a particular job, when you start working on it and accomplish it—then you are successful. Thus you are a success when you decide on something and complete it.

Work is your friend, not your enemy. Every day work hard as if your life depends on it. Work as if it is an exercise regimen, not labour. Work as if all your efforts are 'effortless efforts'. Eventually you will reach a stage where your work will indeed become an effortless effort.

It is not necessary that all the tasks you perform today be interesting. On the path of achieving complete success and the ultimate purpose of success, there will be certain activities that you may find boring. You have to complete them keeping your goal in mind, and very soon every work will become a form of self-expression for you.

Do contemplate on why and how you are doing the things that you do. There is no work in this world that cannot be made into an exercise for the body, mind or intellect. It is better to work as if performing penance like a happy yogi than to toil like a porter.

Let your skills speak through your work. Your work should spell your name and not vice versa. Respect your work. If it's your life, you are also accountable for it. If you hold others responsible for your failures, you may get temporary relief but later on you will come to face much bigger failures.

Through hard work, dedication and perseverance, prepare yourself thoroughly for the goal of complete success. If you try to make your present the best, a bright future will appear before you by default. Instead of building castles in the air, first learn to construct a little hut on solid ground. Else people while away valuable time in airy-fairy talk.

> A boy asked his friend in a serious tone, 'My kite has got entangled in the cables above; what should I do now?' His friend replied, 'Only the Law can help you now. We should call the Law.' Baffled by this reply, the boy asked, 'What does the Law have to do with kites stuck in cables? Why should we call it?' His friend chuckled and said, 'Because the Law has long arms!'

However right and amusing such answers may seem, they are baseless. Such hollow suggestions have never solved anybody's problems. The solution to problems is unearthed by digging like a detective. Being successful is doing and accomplishing that which you had decided.

◆ ◆ ◆

Practical Exercise

Make a list of all the commitments you have made to others that are still incomplete. Having made the list, carry out either of the following actions: complete it or communicate to the concerned person when you will do it or that you will no longer be doing it.

What next?

We shall look at the most important commitment you have to make to yourself in Chapter 7.

7
Impersonal Life

What is the exact meaning of the words 'impersonal life'? The dictionary meaning of the word 'impersonal' is unfriendly or formal or aloof. That is not what is meant here. What we mean by the term 'impersonal life' is leading a life that is not personal or individualistic. Impersonal as opposed to a personal life here refers to an inclusive (as opposed to exclusive) or universal (as opposed to individual) life.

A life lived in the service of Self (Consciousness) is an impersonal life. It is not a selfish life. In fact it is a Self-ish life—a life where the individual ego is transcended and one lives established in the Self. It is the state in which you live for others because there is no other.

An impersonal life leads to happiness

An impersonal life is a life led serving others with the understanding that all are one. When one is established in this consciousness, then every event is seen with different eyes. When the experience of 'I am' is added to anything that is personal, it becomes impersonal. This 'I am' refers to I-amness, the existential experience of consciousness.

> *There was a village where everyone used to wear a cap that had an in-built barometer of happiness. The barometer displayed that person's happiness quotient at the end of the day. Everyone in the village had noticed that the happiness quotient goes up to a maximum of 50%. Usually it was 20%, 25%, 40%, but never above 50%. One day, a villager, who was a seeker by nature, questioned himself that when a potential of 100% happiness exists, then why is it that it never goes above 50%? He began seeking. It is seeking that makes all the difference, not mere wishing. One day he found the answer. His joy knew no bounds. He told the secret to the other villagers. But they did not take him seriously. However, some villagers anyway tried what he said. And they found that their happiness level increased above 50% for the first time. What was the secret? The secret was that whenever you serve anyone else, the barometer of happiness displays a level above 50%.*

This is not somebody else's story. This is *our* story—of each and every one of us. Our level of happiness rises significantly when we live an impersonal life. What we usually experience in personal life is not even half the happiness that we possibly can. An individual celebrates his birthday in pomp and style. He calls celebrities, gets his photos on Page 3 of newspapers, cuts a large cake, eats, dances and makes merry. He does feel happy to some extent. But when he uses his birthday to distribute books to the needy, so as to propagate self-development instead, he finds his level of happiness is much higher than just celebrating a personal birthday.

When you live an impersonal life, you will say leading this way of life is but common sense. It is common sense to lead an impersonal life and be happy. It is a sure method to attain happiness; then why not be more happy and spread happiness by leading an impersonal life? You want water—you go and drink it from the water cooler. This is not rocket science. This is just plain common sense. Similarly, leading an impersonal life is common sense. Not only will you be happier, but all the forces of the universe will come to your aid. People will automatically gather around you to support you. They will respect you and would want to model their lives around you. However, do not let respect and praise be your focus. You automatically get happiness and support from others, but if these are your primary motive, then you have lost your impersonal intention. As Viktor Frankl, a great Austrian psychiatrist, said, 'Success, like happiness, cannot be pursued; it must ensue... as the unintended side effect of one's personal dedication to a cause greater than oneself.'

Make a difference. Aim high, begin small.

When you live an impersonal life, something beautiful happens to your life. There is a law of nature which states that whatever you become a cause for, manifests in your life as well. In fact it multiplies in your life. As Ralph Waldo Emerson has said, 'It is one of the most beautiful compensations in life that no man can sincerely try to help another without helping himself.' Those who heal others, themselves get healed. When you strive to elevate the consciousness of others, your consciousness is elevated. In life, it is what you give that makes the difference, not what you take. Focus on giving, not on taking. Focus on giving love, and love will multiply manifold in your life. Focus on giving money, and money will flow back into your life, manifold.

Take on a high aim, an impersonal aim. Ask yourself, do you really want to be instrumental in achieving that aim? Nature helps those who aim high. All the forces of nature will unify to support you when you aim high to cause an impact in the lives of others. Once you decide on this aim, immediately start working to develop the smaller qualities that will help you to attain your aim.

Keep climbing the smaller mountains you come across until you reach the summit

Many ask, 'How do I start? I do not understand what the purpose of my life is. When an impersonal vision is not clear to me, how do I begin?'

The answer is to begin small. Say, you are working in a company. You are not clear what the impersonal purpose of your life is. In that case, take on any small aim. It does not matter whether you have direction in the beginning. Start working on some cause. For example, start volunteering in an orphanage in your spare time after work. As you climb that mountain, you will discover your calling. You may discover that the orphanage you have begun visiting regularly, actually does not inspire you much. What inspires you is working with children to make them literate. So now start teaching children. Call poor and illiterate children to your home and teach them. Now you are on this next mountain. As you climb this mountain, you may discover another mountain that you are so passionate about that everything else seems trivial. Maybe, as you work on literacy of children, you may discover that your passion is in creating audio-video aids so that all children of the world can easily become literate. You may discover that 'education of children' is your calling. You have now reached a summit wherefrom the view for the next few years is clear. This is what you have to do if your vision is not clear, i.e. take on any vision and work on it. In the process you will discover your calling. You will discover your life's purpose. Perhaps you have to climb two or three mountains to reach your summit, but you will reach there. You will then want to do that full time, and nothing else. Thereafter take the right decision at the right time.

❖ ❖ ❖

Practical Exercise

What is the goal of your life—your individual aim? Reflect on this. What is your organizational vision? In other words, what is the goal of the organization you are a part of? Contemplate on this. Having your aim clearly in writing is a key to success. To generate clarity about your aim, consider performing the following exercise.

Write or type your aim in the following manner:

I am (Part 1)_____who is (Part 2) _____ so that (Part 3) _____ _____.

The answer to Part 1 is who you want to be; your role. Even if you haven't become what you want to be as yet, it is better to write it in the present tense as 'I am' instead of 'I will'. This will help your mind to easily manifest this vision as soon as possible instead of in the distant future. The answer to Part 2 is how you would be doing what you would be doing. The answer to Part 3 is the impact you would have on others or on humanity in general.

Some examples that would emerge are as follows:

- *I am a carpenter, who is the best carpenter in the world building comfortable furniture, so that people can experience higher levels of consciousness comfortably.*
- *I am a CEO, who runs one of the largest IT companies successfully, so that the world can experience innovation and become a better place through technological advancement.*
- *I am a trainer, who is a world class facilitator of leadership and spirituality, so that people can attain a higher level of consciousness.*

What next?

A personal mission takes you toward struggle. An impersonal mission takes you towards peace. In the examples above, which component is most important to you? Is it Part 1, Part 2 or Part 3? If it is Part 1, then you have a clear vision. If Part 2 is most important to you, then you are clear about your mission. If Part 3 is most important to you, then you have an impersonal vision as well as an impersonal mission.

Many people stop at Part 1. They say, 'I will be a doctor.' That's it. Some people aspire more and say they will be the best doctor. But a true leader is one who is clear about the impact his role shall cause to humanity. Let us suppose you say, 'I am a CEO, who runs one of the largest IT companies successfully, so that the world can experience innovation and become a better place through technological advancement.' You shall become what you focus on. If your focus is on the first part of a sentence (I am...), you may end up just being a CEO. You will simply be a role and would have achieved your personal vision. If your focus is on the second part of the sentence (who is...), then you may probably end up playing a key role in a large IT multinational. You may be its CEO too. You would have achieved your mission of running a large IT multinational successfully. This is better than just aspiring to be a CEO. Here your focus is on both a personal vision and a mission—who you shall be and how you shall do it.

But the key is to focus on the third part. All great leaders are great because of their focus on the third part. If your focus is truly on the third part (so that...), then it is an impersonal vision. In the example we are discussing, if your focus is on how the world can experience innovation and become a better place through technological advancement, you shall do anything and everything to make a positive impact on people's lives. If your focus is truly there, it will not matter to you whether you are the CEO or whether you are running a large multinational successfully. All that will matter to you is whether you are causing innovation in the IT field and making the world a better place. Titles and methods just become a means to achieve the end.

If your focus in on the third part, it is an impersonal vision. It is beyond personal. You may end up being the owner or founder, but it does not matter. You may be a facilitator, but it does not matter much. Mahatma Gandhi never aspired to be the Prime Minister or President of a free India. He just aspired for a free India. He didn't worry about who would become the Prime Minister or President. That is why he is considered to be a great leader. What differentiates leaders from great leaders is that leaders have a vision, but great leaders have an impersonal vision. Swami Vivekananda's focus was not on becoming the head of the Ramakrishna Mission or creating more brances of that organization. His vision was that of universal vedanta.

So, as a next step, create your impersonal vision. In Chapter 8, you shall understand the importance of foresight in creating an impersonal vision.

8
Importance of Foresight

As mentioned earlier, even a personal vision propels you to automatically innovate—create and complete. On the other hand, an impersonal vision unleashes your latent innovation power totally. Thus, creating an impersonal vision is most critical to expand yourself and unleash innovation naturally.

Creating a vision means defining your future possibilities through foresight. Assessing the future with the outlook of farsightedness. The one who can anticipate the future situation based on his present, prepares himself for it in advance. If he foresees that ten years down everything will be computerized, he will start learning how to use the computer right from today. Foresight is an essential quality needed to be successful. Develop this quality and prepare yourself for the future possibilities. This way you will be successful today and tomorrow as well. This quality will save you from failure. You shall be alert and ready for any possibility.

For example, if you start getting aches, pains or other symptoms in your body, then with foresight you will understand that such problems may increase with age. To avoid the possibility of developing a chronic illness you will start exercising today. Ideally, instead of beginning exercise after experiencing pain, you should start it much in advance.

Create your vision with foresight

All successful people of the world have this quality of foresight and therefore have a vision. Based on where society is headed today, they anticipate what will happen after ten years and then think of what they should do today to ensure that after ten years they lead a grand life and not a miserable one. You must think now about how you can be happy then too. You have to start working in that direction today. Then you will see in the future that everybody else will be complaining but you are calm because through foresight you had seen the upcoming problems and have already found the solution to them. Only a judicious and farsighted person can think in this manner. Even though it does not appear to be so important today, he certainly sows some seeds for his future while continuing with his current activities. It may seem to others that the time has not yet arrived for it and it is not essential today, but he knows how important it is for his present and his future.

You will find many examples of emperors in history who had keen foresight. Only those kings and kingdoms prospered. For example, some could anticipate the need of a better water supply system in view of the rising population. To avoid scarcity in the future, they began managing the water supply innovatively. They started the work of bringing tributaries of big rivers to their kingdoms so that in 10-20 years, when the population would have increased, the work would be done. Only such visionary leaders can work best for the society.

After looking with foresight at the future, you do not have to start worrying that after 10 or 20 years so-and-so problems may arise. Foresight is not for worrying. Foresight is for understanding what changes need to be done in our present activities. As soon as you get signals through your foresight, you have to bring about changes in your work today. Whatever you are doing now, you have to do it best. Alongside, continue bringing about minor changes in your activities. If your present becomes best, your future automatically turns out to be the best.

The quality of foresight is not present in the unsuccessful, lazy and dull individual. He can neither assess the present situation, nor is he capable of predicting the future based on the present. Such a person always finds himself to be inadequate in the future. He can barely manage two square meals a day after a lot of sweat. He neither contemplates nor thinks about improving his qualities. The only thing he can do best is to curse others. You are reading this book because you desire to achieve success. Practise using your foresight and based on it start working on increasing your capability.

❖ ❖ ❖

Practical Exercise

Refine the impersonal vision you have created in the previous chapter. Use foresight to add to your impersonal vision. Contemplate on what the future shall be in 5-10 years from now. Accordingly modify your impersonal vision statement.

What next?

In Chapter 9, you shall learn more about how you can bring impersonal vision to whatever you are doing now.

9
Living for others because there is no other

Serving others, with the understanding that there is no other, is the ultimate purpose of success. Hence it's not that you have to begin to work on an impersonal project just in your spare time. It's not that you have to do something impersonal only after work. Even if the nature of your work seems personal, it can be converted into an impersonal work by adding an impersonal intention.

Supposing you are a shopkeeper who sells television sets. You may wonder what impersonal intentions you can add to that. One simple intention is to think that you are not just selling idiot boxes, but you are into selling entertainment equipment that bring joy and even knowledge into the lives of all family members—young and old. Still better would be to convert this impersonal intention into an impersonal cause. You can proactively create some stickers which remind viewers not to get too attached to what they are watching and paste them on each television set in an aesthetic manner. You can print schedules of programs that teach something good to children and adults and pass them on to your consumers. You can even start a regular newsletter that updates your consumer community about consciousness elevation programs. Thus, in whatever you do or sell, you can add an impersonal vision. Of course, if you are selling liquor, you may not be able to add an impersonal intention. Do not add an impersonal intention for namesake. Do not say that I am selling liquor and even drinking is a form of happiness. Liquor does not elevate consciousness, it depletes it. Thus your choice of profession is also important. Choose a profession where it is easier to express the impersonal.

Whatever you are doing in your current job or profession, open your mind and ask yourself, how can I make this impersonal? Do not be limited in your thinking—that all profits should come to me alone, that things should happen only in this particular way, etc. A creative solution can be found for everything.

Impersonal vision in the corporate world

In the corporate world, there is already a practice of creating a vision statement and ensuring strategies flow from that vision. But not many corporates take on an impersonal vision. Some corporates do state an impersonal vision but may not implement it in earnest. What makes a difference is the clarity regarding the impact your vision has on people. Leadership theory is abound with the wisdom that the organizational vision needs to be inspiring and noble. Mr. Narayan Murthy, known for achieving heights of corporate success, and one of India's leading visionaries says, 'You have to create a grand, noble vision, which elevates the energy, enthusiasm and self-esteem of everyone in the company, while ensuring that everybody sees a benefit in following the vision.'

It's not that such an impersonal vision needs to be top-down. Every corporate team, however small they may be or however down they may be in their hierarchy, can link their corporate objectives to an impersonal vision.

Let us assume that a corporate team has the objective of executing a software project in three months' time. If the team has to be fully inspired, the first step the team needs to ask itself is: 'What is the difference we shall create in the world through this software project? What would be the impact of this project on people?' If they realize that one key objective is that thousands of employees and customers would be benefitted and their productivity will go up, then they have expanded their narrow vision to an impersonal vision. Thus productivity of people going up really becomes the vision—whether the project is successful or not. They may then include those features in the software that they had not thought about earlier. They may also decide to write a research paper about how they designed the project so that it is helpful for others. They may decide to give away certain ideas free of cost to others so that the world can benefit. When corporate teams link their objectives to an impersonal vision, then they have given themselves a purpose.

Let us assume there is another team whose sole purpose is to produce a financial report in a month's time. Again, that team should ask itself, 'What is the higher purpose in this? Is there an impersonal vision therein?' They may realize that their impersonal vision is that through this project they shall train themselves in principles of finance so that their company benefits. They may realize that they can take on the additional objective of coaching friends and colleagues on the principles of finance after completion of the project.

This is the first step. It could seem a difficult one. Many corporate teams would not want to tread this path. They may find it a path less travelled. But then they remain just teams. Not leading teams. Why is it that during the freedom struggle of any nation, people come together and work so amicably and later on after achieving freedom begin squabbling? Till they achieved freedom, they had a noble purpose. Hence even if having an impersonal vision is a road less travelled, corporate teams can consider it. When a person sees others' eyes are closed, he wishes to close his eyes too and follows the beaten path. Let your presence be such that others open their eyes in your presence.

Impersonal vision in families

Every family can create an impersonal vision statement and implement it. At the minimum, family members can have the goal of promoting the spiritual growth of each other. When every family member is committed for each other's spiritual growth, then they have moved beyond personal to impersonal to some extent. If families can collectively decide to do good for the society by championing a cause, they have then moved further. Move beyond paltry aspirations and focus on the impersonal. Let limited thinking and meagre desires you may have in family life not come in the way of unlimited possibilities and enormous Self-expression. If members of a family are focused on personal issues such as, 'Everyone should respect me; everyone should respect my time; nobody should interfere in my activities…', then they do not progress towards the impersonal vision.

One easy way of being focused on each other's consciousness elevation in families is to pray for the spiritual growth of each other. Pray for all the members of your family, no matter how they behave with you.

Another powerful way of bringing an impersonal focus to your family life is by inspiring your children. When parents work on eliminating their own harmful tendencies and grow as complete individuals, children automatically imbibe this quality and follow suit. Untrained parents lead to untrained children. Children learn through observation. The best gift you can give your children is that you should always be happy—always at a high level of consciousness. Thereby they grow up as highly evolved children. They grow up assuming that this is how life is meant to be lived—happily and peacefully. Another great gift parents can give their children and thereby serve the world is to inculcate in children the habit of fulfilling their commitments. Again, when children see parents being true to their word, they will learn to do the same. Such children grow up to be reliable and self-reliant. For this to happen, parents have to demonstrate that once they give a commitment to anybody, they fulfil it without any reminders. Any amount of preaching will not be as powerful as a child's first-hand experience of seeing his or her parents *do* what they *say*. It is then easy for your child to develop the habit of always being happy and committed to his or her word. Children are an opportunity for you to express your unconditional love. Let your unconditional and pure love for your children motivate you to work on yourself so as to inspire them. Contemplate on how you can raise your child in a way that he or she can be of great service to the world.

◆◆◆

Practical Exercise

Decide what you can do now to take on an impersonal vision in your work and family.

What next?

Your career, job or profession takes a fantastic shape once you identify an impersonal vision and pursue it. Then money and other resources become mere vehicles to support you to attain your impersonal vision. As you practise living an impersonal life, you will start getting free from thoughts of I, me, myself. The moment you become fully free from these words or concepts, you are liberated. That is the journey from ego to egoless. As you live for others because there is no other, it becomes important to learn how to speak to others so as to inspire them for an impersonal vision. This is what we shall see in Part III.

Part III

Success in the realm of saying

Untie the Natural Communicator within you

10
Communication for Self-Expression

A word once uttered and an arrow once shot can never be taken back. They either strike success or inflict destruction.

Man has been empowered with the power of speech, which is the second realm you have to work upon. The words uttered by you create a spectrum of energy, in the way *mantras* do. The vibration of negative words has a damaging effect on you; there are even physical ramifications to it. Positive words create a vibration that produces beautiful results.

When language was not born as yet, there were neither words nor thoughts. People in those times related to things on the basis of feelings in their heart. With the need for language, there came words. And with words, there came thoughts. Now, through words, thoughts can be altered. And through thoughts, feelings can be altered. The vibration of every word has the power to either rejuvenate your health or push you down the mire of illnesses.

Use words with care. Be aware of what you say and work on the words and lines that you tend to use, if you want complete success. Look back on your choice of words in daily activities. When you want to tell someone 'Don't shout!', you can instead say 'Speak softly'. You will see the effect that such positive words have on your body as well as others'. Positive vibrations of your words will begin to help you. Instead of saying 'Don't slam the door', you can say 'Close it gently'. You say the same thing but in a positive manner. It will give you pleasant results.

Parents often complain that their children don't listen to them. But they do not realize that they themselves use negative language with children. Children are quick to form images in their mind about what is being said to them. When you say words like 'don't shout' or 'don't bang', an image of violence is created in their brain, which affects them negatively. Hence it is very important that you start using positive language with children.

In olden days, people walked the path of Truth and hence their words carried tremendous power. The words uttered by them in anger would turn into a curse and manifest in reality. But in today's era, words are losing their potency due to extensive misuse. Backbiting, abusive language, criticism and lies are gradually sucking out the power from words. Now you have to regenerate that power by using positive words.

When troubled by fear of failure, go into a meditative state and repeat this line to yourself: 'I am God's property; my success is assured.' Recitation of these words will generate power within you. When you say these words with assertion, a field of positive vibration is created around you, which pulls success towards you from wherever it is. Such is the power of words.

Words should be used cautiously as they carry enormous power. Think about the words you should use when you convey your thoughts to people. In the midst of conversation, you sometimes speak words that produce negative vibrations. You sometimes use phrases that have a negative undertone. Repetition of such words has a negative effect on you. Even words used jokingly affect you and the people around. Our subconscious mind does not understand jokes; it takes in the literal meaning of words.

For example, if a person chastises his assistant every day by saying 'You are a pain in the neck!', then after a while he actually develops a pain in his neck. We don't even know that the words that we habitually use affect us in a major way. We have to be alert about their usage and avoid them. If someone has a habit of saying 'My blood boils when I see him... he is a big headache... I don't want to see him at all...', it would be no surprise if he indeed develops high blood pressure, headache or eye problems.

The power of words will help us achieve success if we bring about a positive change in our talk. Man offers prayers to God and sings hymns in His praise, because they are filled with the power of words. And this power has a beneficial effect on him. Words coming out of your mouth affect you first, and then others. Therefore use this power judiciously, lest it becomes a bane instead of a boon.

Choose your words carefully

If your focus is on what you have lost, you will always remain unhappy. If your focus is on what you have gained, you will always remain happy. A happy man can never hurt anyone.

Generally, when you buy some expensive item, you tend to say, 'Here go my thousands of rupees...' But now you have to shift your focus to what you have gained. You should say, 'I've got myself a great utility item today which will not only give me comfort but also save my time and energy.' When you purchase an exercise equipment, instead of saying that you had to spend so much money to buy it, you should say to yourself, 'I now have the equipment and the technique to achieve good health.' Learn this art of choosing your words while saying them to others or to yourself (self-talk).

In his ignorance, man repeatedly utters negative sentences, like: 'I can't succeed; I don't have the determination to win... Money is hard to come by; if it comes it doesn't stay; if it stays my friends turn into rivals... If I give someone my time, money or help, I won't be left with much... Good times and good things don't last forever; hence we should be prepared for bad times... Nobody loves me... Alas! If only my parents had loved me... I'll have to go through the same that my friends and relatives did... Learning is difficult and I take a lot of time to learn... Illness is in my blood... I am born to suffer at the hands of others... I am always a victim of bad weather...'

The day your words brim with faith and wisdom, your self-talk will change into something like: 'Free time is not meant for boredom, it is an opportunity to think creatively and discover something... God has provided everything in abundance; I am blessed with abundant love, money, time, happiness, health and contentment... Life loves me and wants to see me successful... My mind overflows with divine thoughts; hence success is easy for me...'

Some people do want success but fear the responsibility that comes with it. This fear creates a tendency in their body to fall sick so that responsibility can be evaded. Children often fall sick just before their examinations. If you too have similar problems, start affirming to yourself: 'I am ready for change. Success is safe for me. Life loves me and wants to see me completely successful. I have only divine thoughts in my mind. I have faith in life. Fear and insecurity are mere clouds that come and go; I can see the moon (my goal) even behind these clouds.'

If you eliminate all negative words from your talk, you will be amazed to find that nobody is able to make you fail or make you sad. People get dejected on facing criticism and abandon their quest for complete success. At such times, affirm to yourself: 'Sticks and stones can break my bones but words can cause me no harm. I cannot let myself become unhappy upon facing criticism.'

Free yourself from the mesh of old, stale words. Learn to use new positive words and feelings. Let not others' behaviour dampen you. When you are sad, you get thoughts of only hopelessness and worry. Whenever that happens, say to yourself, 'I am allowing myself to feel sad and hopeless.' If you can allow yourself to feel sad and hopeless, it means you can also allow yourself to feel happy and cheerful. This will snap you into awareness and your sorrow will be alleviated. You will own up to the responsibility of keeping yourself happy. In this way you will light a new lamp of hope inside you.

❖❖❖

Practical Exercise

Say the following words out loud with all your heart. Let these words reverberate in you and you can then observe their impact. 'I have quit complaining, I have no grudge against anyone. I have total faith in life; I am ready to go with the flow of life with complete acceptance. I love and accept myself. I lovingly take care of my body and mind. Everything in my life happens at the right time, in the right way. I am free from thoughts of the past and future, I live in the present. I will always continue with the positive thought pattern that has produced this joy inside me. I have every right to achieve complete success.'

You can definitely find some of the above words inspiring. In difficult times, you can also reiterate these words: 'God is with me. He is compassionate. He helps me and guides me at the right time. Whatever God does is always good for me.' When you say these words with faith, every difficulty will leave you with some lesson, some knowledge and a lot more confidence.

What next?

Having understood the power of words, let us understand how to untie the natural communicator within you.

11
Powerful Personality for Self-Expression

For complete success, it is important to learn natural self-expression. You can work years on improving your communication skills, but if you are not aware of the missing link of self-expression, you may end up focusing on just impressing people. There is no need to impress; just express.

How to naturally untie the communicator within to access the power of self expression? For that, write down the answers to the questions below. It is important that you first write and only then read ahead.

Q1. How do you define personality? Is personality the way you look? Is personality the way you talk? The way you walk? Pause for a while and note down your definition of personality.

Q2. Please rate your personality on a scale of 1-10. Here 1 will be indicative of very poor and 10 excellent.

Q3. According to you, what should have happened in your childhood or in your past so that you could have rated yourself at 10? (If you have already rated yourself at 10, then you need not answer this question.)

Q4. What can you do now to improve your personality? What actions will you take so as to be able to rate yourself at 10? How can you further improve if you have rated yourself at 10?

Q5: How much time will it take for you to implement the changes you have mentioned in your answer to Q4, in order to build a powerful personality?

Now that you have encountered these questions, let us define personality. Personality is simply defined as what you think about yourself, or in other words, what you believe yourself to be. This is also called self-image.

You may think that your appearance and presentation is your personality. Looks, dressing, etc. may have some effect on your personality, but personality is mainly shaped by what you think about yourself. If you think you have a strong personality, others are going to receive that message subconsciously and thereby regard you as a strong personality. If you think you have a weak personality, guess what others will think about you? They too shall consider you as a weak person, however good you may look. It is what you think about yourself that matters.

What personality is not

Examine your answer to Q1. Have you mentioned that looks determine personality? The fact is that personality has very little to do with looks. There are innumerable examples of those who don't score high in appearance and yet have a powerful personality. Be it Gandhi, Lincoln, or Mother Teresa, their personality was powerful mainly because of the supreme self-belief they had. There are numerous sports celebrities, who are not tall or handsome, yet they have a great personality. There are many character actors or businessmen who are too thin or too stout or bald—yet they have won the Oscar Award or Best Business Personality Award.

If your looks have played a role in not rating yourself at 10 on the personality score question (Q2), then you are harbouring a wrong belief. Examine your answer to Q3. Have you answered that I should have been born more beautiful or handsome? Tell yourself that it is a wrong belief. Even if you have not written this, does the thought that you are not very handsome or beautiful bother you in your day to day life? Again, tell yourself: looks have nothing to do with my personality. It is a belief. And a belief can be dropped. Just understand what personality is not about and what it is mainly about.

Your bank balance or education also have very little to do with your personality. There are countless examples of social workers who are penniless but possess a powerful personality. There are plenty of examples of those who did not have a good education and yet have a great personality. Once again examine your answers to Q3 especially. Have you said that in the past I should have studied more? Do you think, 'If only I were richer, I would have a great personality'? Is such thinking reflected in your answer to Q3? Once again these are just false beliefs.

Interestingly, personality is also not about how good a communicator you are. It is also not about the knowledge you have. There are once again many examples of those who are good speakers but have a poor personality. Their knowledge gives them an edge in speaking. But yet when you meet them, you don't feel good. You don't feel good because they don't feel good inside. What they think about themselves gets transmitted.

Personality is just what you think yourself to be

Examine your answer to Q4. If personality is simply what you think yourself to be, how can you improve it? The answer is simple. You need not 'do' anything to improve it. You already have a great personality. You just need to 'think' and 'believe' so. Just thinking and believing that you have a great personality is enough. And this is not a false belief. Who you are—your essence—is unlimited and great in every way. It is the source of all creation. A happy natural state is your essence. Doesn't every child have a great personality? Isn't every child a great communicator? This is because a child is untouched by ego or insecurities. Personality is just what you think yourself to be—your self-image. When you believe this, you will be amazed that by just dropping all beliefs about personality and holding on to a thought that you have a great personality, people around you reciprocate too.

Examine your answer to Q5. How much time will it take to improve your personality? If you have truly understood this chapter, then it will take no time. The list that you have written—*'I shall improve my communication and then my personality will improve, I shall improve this or that and then my personality will improve'*—is the problem. The list is the problem. It stops you. The list is a set of reasons because of which you keep saying that one day you shall have a great personality. Just understand that personality is what you think yourself to be. Change your thoughts about yourself. It takes a moment to change your thoughts. It will reflect on your personality. Then your self-expression and its impact on others will be simply amazing.

❖❖❖

Practical Exercise

Mentioned below are a few statements about self-confidence. Tick what is true for you and what is false for you:

- *I don't look good. That is why I don't have a good personality.*

- *If only I was taller; if only I was fair-skinned; if only I had a good physique, then I would have had a good personality.*

- *I don't speak good English and hence I don't have a good personality.*

- *I am poor in communication skills.*

- *It takes years to develop a good personality.*

- *I am not confident.*

- *Others laugh at me.*
- *I don't make a good impression on others.*
- *Communication is about good verbal and written skills.*

What next?

Having read this chapter, you would have understood that all the statements mentioned in the practical exercise are myths. If you still consider any of them to be true, drop them through contemplation or deep thinking. Since thinking has such a profound impact on our words and actions, let us see how to achieve success in the realm of thinking in the following section.

Part IV

Success in the realm of thinking

Unravel the Natural Achiever within you

12
Self-Elevation for Productivity

Man is the only living being which possesses the skill of language and therefore the power to think. In human beings, thoughts arise and dissolve incessantly. Just like your breath that goes on automatically, thoughts too go on automatically. And just as in *pranayam*, where you control the inflow and outflow of your breath to the count of 4 (or whatever you have decided for yourself), you can do the same with your thoughts as well. With a little practice and a little understanding, you can give a direction to your thoughts. If you do not steer your thoughts, they will steer and control you.

In the absence of a direction, various kinds of thoughts run indiscriminately through one's mind. Such thoughts often stink of fear and worry. For instance, 'I don't know what tomorrow holds for me... What if I am sacked from my job...? What will I do when I get old or fall sick...? Will my children forget me after they get married...?' Doubts, scepticism and uncertainty plague an individual's mind relentlessly, and he dies every moment, every day of his life. Unhappiness is but inevitable. As soon as one thought falls, another one rises. As one thought of misery ends, another one shapes up. A vicious circle of unhappiness gathers around. Unless you orient your thoughts explicitly, they will continue their onslaught unabated. If you don't give them a direction, the blessing of thinking power turns into a curse.

You have no idea of the things you are attracting towards yourself with the power of your thoughts. Hence you give even negative thoughts a free entry into your mind. Things come into your life purely because of your thoughts. It is only your thoughts that attract the kind of incidents that occur in your life. It is therefore crucial for you to always maintain a positive outlook before beginning any task. Give yourself the auto-suggestion: 'I am God's child. My success is assured.' When you have positive thoughts, your brain works its best. When your thoughts are negative or irritable, your intellect ebbs down and becomes listless.

Do not waste the power of thinking in lowly thoughts. The majestic power of your intellect should not be used for taking undue advantage of the weak. People who employ inappropriate means for making profits often plummet into the depths of failure. Nature has blessed us with profound intellect, and we must utilize it for creative and constructive thinking. Seeking our true self (self-realization) is also a part of such thinking.

The thoughts that we harbour in turn attract more of similar thoughts. And this cumulative energy of thoughts creates either a glorious palace for us or sorry ruins.

Make right use of the power of thoughts

There is unfathomable power in your thoughts. They can produce either a positive or a negative impact on your life. It is up to you to decide how to utilize this power. Some people, out of ignorance, use this power for trivial gains.

> *Once a boy found a penny while walking down the road. From then on, he got into the habit of looking down while walking, in*

hope of finding some more coins. He never looked up at the sky after that day. Thus for the sake of his petty desire, he lost out on the whole sky.

The power present in positive thoughts creates a positive vibration within you, and this vibration attracts all things positive towards you. Happy thoughts bring joy into your life. It does not matter in which direction the front door of your house opens, north-south or east-west, but always be aware of the direction of your thoughts.

When you think negative, such as, 'I cannot do this work', you put a full stop to your thought process. But when you think positive, like, 'Let me see how I can go about this job', you give your intellect a chance to think. Positive thoughts open up new avenues for your intellect to grow and evolve. If you need to buy something but your mind moans, 'I cannot afford to buy it', flip the thought and think of *how* you can buy it. This will set you on the right track and you will strike upon the appropriate method. The influence of optimistic thoughts will add tremendous pace to your journey towards success.

In the beginning, each and everything triggers negative thoughts. The mind has the habit of seeking out the negative in everything it sees. You will always spot the one little dark speck on an otherwise snow-white wall. You fail to see the whiteness that is all around you. This is the habit of the mind. It is so important to train the mind. Every child learns to breathe by himself, but then why is he taught *pranayam*, the technique of controlling the flow of breath? It is because he is not familiar with this technique; he needs to learn it. Similarly you need to be trained in controlling the direction of thoughts that run in and out all day long.

We are quick to spot that tiny dark speck, but why cannot we see the entire white wall? Why cannot we see the entire sky? Why do only the moon and the stars grab our attention when the whole open sky beckons us? Observe yourself and see: What are your thoughts like from morning to night? What thoughts do various events evoke in you? Do you see only the black spot or can you see the whole white wall too? Do you always think of the one tooth you have lost or do you remember that you have 31 solid teeth firmly in place? Where is your attention focused? If you are able to stay positive in your thoughts, the roots of success will spread and strengthen in your life.

> *A teacher scoffed at a student in class. 'You are a dimwit. You will never achieve anything in life.' This remark had such an impact on the student's psyche that before beginning any work, his mind would pop up only one thought: 'I won't be able to do this.' As a result none of the work that he undertook ever reached a satisfactory conclusion. Just one negative thought ruined his life. This is a fact with most people. A single negative thought leads them to believe that they can never be successful, but this is not so, at all. Somebody only needs to change their thoughts to: 'Yes, you can do whatever you want to.' That's it. Just this one thought can transform their life.*

Every thought turns into reality. EVERY THOUGHT IS A PRAYER EMERGING FROM INSIDE YOU. And every prayer yields fruit—sometimes quickly and sometimes after a while. If all the great men, philosophers and saints of this world are not wrong, you must immediately replace your negative thoughts with positive ones. You can keep this intention every day in your mind: 'Today, I will not entertain a single negative thought.' You have to observe a fast by abstaining from negative thoughts.

When you are observing this fast, you have to catch yourself thinking negative. You have to be alert enough to spot every little negative thought that arises. When you spot one, you have to halt it and remind yourself of your resolution. No matter how tiny the negative thought may be, it feeds on your mind and becomes stout, and subsequently difficult to dislodge.

Some examples are: 'My colleagues are not cooperating with me today', 'What if there's a power cut in the middle of my work?', 'My boss is surely going to scream at me', 'Looks like I'm in for a long day at work', 'Today's day doesn't seem to be very good', 'I'm getting bored', 'What if I get stuck in the elevator?', 'Will somebody steal my shoes kept outside the temple?', 'What if my bike gets punctured?', 'There'll definitely be a traffic jam ahead', 'The shop will be closed before I get there', 'The movie is going to be a drag', 'My cell phone might get stolen', 'My family is going to be upset with me', 'I am feeling sick', 'Am I going to catch a cold today?', 'The inflation is getting to me', 'I won't be able to do this job', 'What if I fail?', 'All my tasks take a long time to complete', so on and so forth. All these little thoughts are mischievous children of the devil. If you encourage them even for a few moments, they will come and stand before you every day. If you observe a fast and abstain from negative thoughts, these naughty kids will gradually pass off and stop appearing.

Negative thoughts and precautionary thoughts

Understand the difference between negative thoughts and precautionary thoughts. To prepare yourself for an impending calamity is precaution. But to erode from within with apprehensions of a calamity is negative thinking. Locking your car is precaution but fearing that your car might be stolen is negative thinking. Do not fear, only exercise caution.

Those who recognize the power of thoughts encourage only positive ones and sideline negative ones wilfully. If you observe, we are seldom aware of the kind of thoughts that we feed our mind with. It is important that we filter our thoughts. We borrow a lot of thoughts from the television, newspapers, movies, friends and other people. Are we leading our lives taking those thoughts to be the truth? Or are we using our own power of thinking? This question will raise your awareness about your thoughts.

Like a guard at the gates, examine every thought before allowing it inside your mind. Thoughts are food of the mind. Check whether the food is healthy. If it is harmful for your mind's health, reject it straightaway. Do not encourage harmful thoughts. Do not consider them to be the truth. Laugh at such thoughts; it will kill their spirit.

Starting today, if you maintain positive, Truthful and Divine thoughts consistently for a period of time, then the creative power of such thoughts will reap miracles in your life. A feeling of wonder will engulf you. The journey of complete success begins with prayer (in the form of your thoughts) and ends in wonder. When you reach the destination, you are left with nothing but astonishment at God's handiwork. 'What a creation this world is...! How beautifully is this game of life being played...! How every body-mind mechanism is being operated by the power of thoughts...!!'

Visualize your thoughts

Before you begin with anything great that you wish to achieve in life, see it happening in your thoughts first. Visualize all your actions on the screen of your mind. Whether you want to cultivate a good quality or wish to come up with a new invention, first of all feel and experience the state of success where you have accomplished it. This feeling will generate an energy, a vibration, that will spread throughout the universe and bring the required quality, event or object to your feet. To achieve success in life, you have to learn the knack of orienting your directionless thoughts. When you firmly infuse the fundamental thought process of achieving success, mental peace and holistic health in your brain so that it becomes ingrained, you will then be able to build a strong foundation for the tower of complete success.

The energy to be successful

An airplane engine subjected to excessive stress begins to wear out resulting in loss of energy. Similarly we need to employ our engine, i.e., our mind suitably according to time and situation. Our mind too starts draining if put through excessive stress. Before the stress develops into a mental illness, the mind should be calmed down. Then you can take the flight of success using a smaller amount of energy.

An airplane consumes a lot of energy while taking off, but upon reaching a particular height, it gains more speed with much lesser energy. Isn't this a wonder?

To take off with your flight of success, understand this rule of energy. Do not waste your energy by getting disheartened over petty matters. Do not let dirt accumulate in the engine of your mind. Keep it clean by forgiving people and cleansing your heart.

While learning to write, little children unnecessarily apply a lot of pressure on the pencil, resulting in undue stress on their entire body. Gradually they pick up the required skills and learn how to write using lesser energy. Similarly you should learn to achieve success by using the least possible energy. This will allow you to use the remainder of your energy to spread your joy of complete success among others and in helping them achieve it too. This is the ultimate purpose of complete success.

People aspiring for success always need to be careful about not dissipating their energy in futile matters. A right balance needs to be achieved in the accumulation and usage of energy. When you engage in arguments, you waste not only your time but your energy as well. Had the same energy been put to use in proper channels, it would have reaped its fruit in the form of success. Wasting energy indiscriminately is as good as inviting failure. Therefore utilize it judiciously. Do not waste it by needlessly indulging in fights, hatred, jealousy, false pride, anger and comparison with others.

A person aiming for success never takes part in any arguments or pointless discussions. If he finds himself amidst such a situation, he questions himself whether these arguments are more important than his goal. He knows the answer instantly and elevates his level of consciousness. In fact he also inspires others to stay away from it. On the other hand, the unaware and unsuccessful person never realizes that in such arguments we gain less and lose more. By indulging in such activities he loses even the little that he had.

When others try to demean a successful person, he avoids confrontation with them to conserve his energy. Thus the successful always remains successful and every failure coming towards him fails to reach him.

❖❖❖

Practical Exercise

Now that you have understood the importance of thoughts, resolve in your mind: 'I will definitely be successful. I will achieve complete success—complete in all respects.' Having resolved so, create a picture of your impersonal vision and see it in your mind's eye regularly.

What next?

Before we come to a unique way to propel your thoughts towards success in Chapter 14, if there is one habit of thinking you have to develop, it is that of Self Analysis. This is what we shall learn in the ensuing chapter.

13
The Habit of Self-Analysis

In his unconsciousness and in his spare time, man commits a lot of mistakes due to which success eludes him. One has to turn inwards and investigate these mistakes. By writing in your diary, you can do a self-analysis to see what mistakes you knowingly or unknowingly commit in your day-to-day activities. By doing a self-check once every week, you should introspect and contemplate over your mistakes so that you do not repeat the same mistakes again. New mistakes indicate progress; old mistakes convey the same old story of unconsciousness.

Maintaining a diary is an excellent method to learn and make headway in life. If you haven't developed this habit yet, it's a good idea to begin right now. And the first thing you should write in it is: *I will write in my diary every day.*

Investigate and bring your flaws to light through self-analysis. A successful person leaves no stone unturned in seeking out his own flaws. Like a detective, he traces out his imperfections. On the other hand when it comes to self-praise, he shows indolence and acts like a novice. Nobody can achieve success by hiding one's shortcomings from oneself. A successful person asks people about his deficiencies. Normally no one likes to hear about one's deficiencies from others, but unless you know about them, how can you improve upon them? There are some faults that you cannot realize on your own but which can be observed by colleagues, family and people around you. If you really want to overcome your deficiencies and learn from your mistakes, you shall seek a feedback from them.

When people learn a new language, there comes an important phase during their learning and gaining expertise in it. Until they assure themselves that 'committing errors is fine', they cannot open up and learn.

Unless they give themselves permission to make mistakes, they cannot advance. But as soon as they accept that making mistakes is okay, they find themselves speaking the language much better and much more fluently. Until they pass through this phase, all their attention is on their errors. And the more they focus on their errors, the more errors they make. The moment they accept their errors, they find themselves free from their clutches. As a result they find a remarkable improvement in their language skills.

Once you accept your mistakes, you find that everything works to your advantage. This is because your attention shifts from 'what is wrong?' to 'what can be done now to improve the situation?' Your mental state becomes clear and relaxed. You begin to see new dimensions of every situation which you couldn't see before. The haze covering the entire scenario begins to clear. Your irritability dissolves and you get relieved from your unsteady state of mind.

It is a great virtue to be able to learn from one's own mistakes. Now that you have understood the purpose of imbibing this virtue, what's next? Now choose new virtues. Take the challenge and start working. To develop a new quality, you must first ask yourself honestly, 'Do I really want to adopt this quality or do I want it so that others form a good opinion about me?' If you have an intense desire to inculcate any virtue, think of all the minute aspects that you need to work upon. This thought process is the tool to excavate the goldmine of virtues.

For example, if you want to become a successful singer, you will have to get up early in the morning and practise the nuances of singing. Along with this you will have to work on a lot of other things, but the practise of music is the primary requirement. Likewise, when you want to nurture a virtue, think of how you can make a small beginning. Let it be as small as a minute or two, but begin doing it. These small decisions go a long way in helping you cultivate the virtue you wish to acquire.

People often make time an excuse. They don't have time to do anything different other than their daily routine. They forget that time travels on unstoppably. Time will keep flying past and you will keep finding excuses. That is why you must begin with developing some small habits that will help you to acquire new qualities.

Continue your investigation as a detective. Find out which qualities all successful people around the world have, due to which they could easily achieve success. Taking up responsibility, making right decisions at the right time and honouring commitments are the three magical virtues that every successful person possesses. These are the foundational virtues for achieving success. If you are able to cultivate these virtues, acquiring any other virtue will be easy for you.

As you analyze yourself further, you will be able to take decisions in accordance with your conscience. A completely successful person listens to his heart or conscience for taking decisions. His decisions are always taken in the larger interest of people. He does only what his conscience feels right. This is the practical rule for achieving the ultimate purpose of success. By taking such higher decisions, he not only wins cooperation and admiration from others but also remains free from any kind of guilt.

A greedy person is habituated to adopting fraudulent means for achieving what he wants, and in doing so, he turns a deaf ear to his inner voice. As a result he loses the support and love of people. He remains miles away from success.

An important secret of success is: Clearly describe to yourself what you want. Then look around to see who already has it. On finding that person, ask him about it, and then by getting in touch with your higher consciousness, make a decision and implement it.

The one who really aspires for success always listens with rapt attention to people of higher consciousness. And even when people having low levels of consciousness speak to him, he never cuts them off mid-sentence. He learns from every person. But he spends more time in the company of awakened people. Consequently, achieving big success comes quite easily to him.

A foolish and unsuccessful person cannot hold himself from constant blabbering. While speaking he learns less and forgets more. He does not like to listen, unaware of the fact that one learns and retains more only by listening. He dislikes being with people who possess a higher level of consciousness than him. He tries to stay in his comfort zone as much as possible. When a seemingly difficult task comes to him, he labels it as 'impossible' and pulls out one excuse after another. Instead of himself learning the lessons of life, he asks others to learn them.

Answer honestly to what's your motive

For a few days, just before retiring for the night, ask yourself what were your actions in various situations throughout the day, and with what motive did you act so? If you did not do some work assigned to you by a particular person, why didn't you do so? Is it because this person does not satisfy your ego? Or is it because he is a hurdle in the way of your ambitions and aspirations? On the other hand if you did do the work someone told you to do, why did you do it? Is it because you were afraid of that person? Or is it because that person satisfies your ego? Do not hide the reality from yourself. Answer yourself honestly. If you like somebody, then why do you like him? Is it because he does what you tell him to do or is it because of his qualities? If you do not like somebody, then is he really bad or is it just because he is an obstacle in your work? Answer in all seriousness.

When you think honestly, you will find that you work with some expectations and with some ego. You have expectations from your brothers, sisters, spouse, children, colleagues, neighbours and others. You want these expectations to be fulfilled. If they do not fulfil these expectations, they become the reason for your unhappiness and anger. In relationships there should be unconditional love and not expectations. In exchange for this love, you should also not expect name, fame or gratitude. Such love awakens in your heart automatically on understanding the Truth. The ego will consequently shatter.

❖❖❖

Practical Exercise

Let us conduct another very important type of self-analysis. After every hour of the day, ask yourself, 'What is the state of the mind now?' Using the A-L checklist given below, check the state of your mind. In this way, observe yourself every hour.

A: Anger: Feeling of rage on yourself or on others.

B: Boredom: Not being interested in anything.

C: Confusion: Not understanding in spite of explanations.

D: Depression: Feeling of melancholy even without reason.

E: Ego: It is 'I, me, myself'. Taking credit. Self-praise.

F: Fear: Feeling afraid of something. Feeling uncertain.

G: Guilt: Self-criticism. 'Why did I do this?'

H: Hatred: Feeling strongly that the other person is wrong.

I: Ill-will: Wanting to hurt somebody.

J: Jealousy: 'Why don't I have what that person has?'

K: Kindness: Wanting to benefit others. Thinking of how to make others happy.

L: Laziness: Not wanting to do anything. Wanting to sit idle.

See for yourself what happens after this observation for a few days.

What next?

On the hourly self-observation, you may have observed that depending on the positive or negative thinking going on in our mind, how our mental state keeps changing. This shows how fickle and unreliable the mind is. And we become happy or sad depending on this mind! Hence we shall learn a unique method of thinking that will help us to transcend this in the following chapter.

14
Truth Thinking

Beyond positive and negative thinking, there is a higher way of thinking. It is called Truth Thinking. It is extremely powerful and effective and it naturally propels you to your goal of complete success. Let us understand it in detail.

Beyond Positive and Negative Thinking

When we generate or encourage negative thoughts, they begin to manifest through us. When we see negative in people or events, we attract more negativity in our lives. Our feelings immediately become negative and we begin to create a negative reality for ourselves. Being positive and thinking positively has always been recommended to get a new perspective on unpleasant incidents, to help us regain our strength and to move ahead in life.

But there is a flip side to it. Let us suppose you see a shiny, new car on the road and instead of getting unhappy with the old one that you have, you think positively and say, 'I want to and can buy a new car if I reach my financial goals.' But when you check within, underneath this positive thinking there is a negative feeling that says: 'I cannot afford a new car.' This negative feeling has an adverse effect on you. People always have questions such as: 'How can I think positive when such a negative incident occurred in my life? How do I generate positive thoughts?... Even though I think positively, I'm not able to make a definitive change in my life. Though I think positive, but how do I get out of the shell of negative feelings?' Positive thinking is certainly better than negative thinking but you have to add a new dimension to your thoughts in order to bring a true change in your attitude and to your life.

Is there a way to see people, events and life from a perspective beyond the duality of positive and negative? Is there a way to retain your level of consciousness in a negative situation and do something to create a new future? Yes! The *Truth Thinking Technology* allows you to do so. Instead of getting entangled in the *Illusory Truth* and getting trapped in the mire of negative thoughts, you have to see the hidden truth, the hidden Self (Consciousness) behind everything.

Instead of cribbing that it is raining heavily, you must see the hidden sun which is about to rise. Instead of dreading the challenges in your life, you have to see success waiting behind the challenges. You are usually tricked and drawn into the illusory truth. Everything negative that you see around is an illusory truth—be it heavy rains, floods, accidents, sickness, traffic jammed roads, dirty lanes, violence, and so forth. On seeing such things, you begin to think, 'How can I accomplish my work?... Something very bad has happened to me... The government will never become effective... People are careless and do not bother about others... If only this happens... If only my wife changes...'

Indulging in such thinking, you are unaware of the Supreme Truth that wants to unfold and of the qualities of the Self that are waiting to be expressed through you. Your thoughts based on the illusory truth block these from manifesting. How can anything be created in the physical realm unless it is first created by you in the realm of your thoughts? When you are busy in negative thinking, how can you even think of what you want to create? The illusory truth based thoughts keep you away from the innovations that are to be brought onto earth for solving the existing problems.

How to implement the Truth Thinking Technology

Truth Thinking Technology implies that you see the *qualities of the Self* instead of focusing on the illusory truth. You welcome the shining sun, abundant harvest, cleanliness, compassion, etc., which are the qualities of the Self. These are all manifestations of consciousness of God. By doing so, you are inviting those qualities into your life, not only through you but through everyone around you. You focus on the qualities of the Self—love, peace, harmony, courage, etc. By doing so, you come out of the negative feeling as well. There are two steps for applying the Truth Thinking Technology:

Step 1: Tell yourself that this (negativity) is an illusory truth.

Step 2: Invoke the quality of Self by saying 'Thank you for _____.'

As part of the first step, you identify the present negative situation as *illusory truth*. However bad the current situation may be, you refuse to buy in. Even if someone is abusing you, or you have lost money in the stock market, tell yourself, 'This is an illusory truth.' Thoughts like 'How will my work get done? What will happen to my job? People never change' are illusory truths. Even if you have fallen sick, identify it as an illusory truth. Good health is waiting at your doorstep. It wants to come in either with the help of new medicines, healing or a miracle. But when you refuse to see it or acknowledge it, how can it come in? By not getting sucked in by the illusory truth of disease, you invite good health into your life.

When you see and believe in the illusory truths of life, you become like an element which attracts all that is negative. But when you choose to see the Truth of Self, you become a powerful magnet attracting all that is positive and best. And only those who are capable of seeing this are able to bring new things onto earth. You have to be unperturbed to be able to see the Truth; else you get drifted away by the illusory truth.

Just by identifying the situation as illusory truth, you do not allow the situation to cast a spell on you.

At step two, you invoke a particular quality of the Self by saying 'Thank you for _____.' You have to invoke that particular quality of the Self which is the opposite of the negative you are seeing. For example when you go out for a walk and notice something negative, like someone has spoiled a wall by writing something bad on it, identify it as an illusory truth. And say to yourself, 'Everything on earth is a piece of creativity and I am here to see the best of creation. Thank you for creativity.' Creativity is one of the qualities of Self. By doing this, you are invoking this particular quality of Self. You are sowing the seed for the next scene you want to see.

Does this mean you don't take any action?

This does not mean that you should not take any action. You have to take the best step befitting the situation. If you are stuck in a traffic jam, find the best way out. The moment you say 'Thank you for order', you give direction to the positive energies of the universe. If someone is behaving rudely with you, the moment you say in your mind 'Thank You for cooperation', you are invoking that quality of Self in the other person. His behaviour towards you will change, and if you constantly see the Truth (that particular quality of Self in him), he may change forever. Even if you say it once, you begin the process of change.

What we are talking about is not a temporary feel-good solution. This is going to bring a permanent change. This will break all limitations in your thinking. You are invoking the quality of Self by being the Self. When you say 'Thank you for _____', you are sending a signal to the universe that you see only the Truth and consequently the entire universe rallies behind you in order to manifest it. The qualities of the Self start working through you. Nature signals you about the change that has begun through the feeling you experience. You can witness the change in your feeling from negative to positive.

But if you are focusing only on the illusory truth, you are entangling the universal energies and also creating wrong things on earth. What do you think is the reason for wars and world wars? It is the result of the collective thinking of the entire human race on earth. What is everyone thinking today? What kind of illusory truth is everyone seeing? War and terrorism are illusory truths. And people are seeing it. With desire to make money, news channels and newspapers are competing with each other and showing wrong things in exaggeration.

You can be happy at this very moment. Your happiness need not depend on someone or something changing. When you see something good in others, accordingly say 'Thank you for goodness', 'Thank you for perfection', 'Thank you for timely help', 'Thank you for abundance'. This will enhance those qualities in your life. There is enough for everyone on this earth. Every bad thing happening in this world can be stopped. The only thing required from you is to come out of the illusory truth. Everything can be stopped—be it financial crisis, earthquakes, famines, riots, world wars or terrorism. You are responsible for everything happening on this planet and you have the power to change it.

❖❖❖

Practical Exercise

Recollect all the major obstacles in your life. Practice Truth Thinking for each of the obstacles.

What next?

One of the greatest obstacles to success is our habit patterns wherein thought patterns are the source. In the subsequent chapter, we shall discover more ways to overcome patterns besides the practice of Truth Thinking.

15
Overcoming Habit Patterns

The biggest obstacle in achieving success is: our tendencies. Tendencies are the fixed patterns of our body-mind mechanism, our wrong habits and our hardened thought structure.

Depending on the people, environment, events, circumstances, etc., some good and some bad habits develop in you unknowingly. Later these habits become the cause of either your success or failure. Study these habits carefully and work on eliminating them methodically.

It is vital for every person to understand the nature of one's body-mind. In what situations do you react? How do you respond to different situations? Under what kind of circumstances do you lose your composure? When are you able to stay unshaken? If you can observe yourself constantly, very soon you will get rid of bad habits and enhance your good habits.

So now let us know and understand some of the major patterns that inflict us. Identify the ones that hamper you in your quest for success.

Fire Pattern

The first pattern is called the fire pattern. People having this pattern are those who are always hot under the collar. They get irritated about every little issue. These people spew their fury as a matter of habit. It is their ingrained tendency (pattern). They provoke anger in themselves and in others. This pattern leaves them incapacitated to achieve success because all day long they are under the influence of anger. There are some people who sometimes get angry, but people with fire pattern only sometimes do not get angry. There is a Chinese saying: 'Don't open a shop if you cannot control your anger and if you cannot smile.' This implies that even if you open a shop, it's not going to run because of this pattern.

Fear Pattern

People having this pattern are cowards and behave like scared rabbits. A coward is always scared and hesitant. He cannot talk amidst people and always stays behind. Every little thing creates fear in his mind. Most of the thoughts running through his head are that of fear. This pattern is an enemy of success.

Liar Pattern

The liar pattern is the habit of being dishonest. There are some people who lie all the time; it has become a hardened habit. They lie even when there is no reason to do so. Trapped in this habit, people lie even if they do not intend to. And they can't come out of it even if they wish to. To hide one lie, they have to resort to a hundred other lies.

> A person happens to meet a friend in the mall. His friend says, 'It's been a long time since you've paid us a visit, so when are you coming?' The person instantly replies 'I will come over in the evening today', in spite of knowing very well that he won't be going.

Man has become so used to being dishonest that he does not even realize that he is lying. Before saying something, he does not think, 'What is it that I am promising? Will I be able to keep my promise?' If someone asks him 'Do you have some change?', he snaps back with a 'No, I don't.' This happens unknowingly. With a little awareness, he could have given a better reply such as, 'I have some change but I cannot give it to you because I need it myself.' But since lying has become a pattern, wrong words just flow out unconsciously.

Blaster Pattern

A person having the blaster pattern initially goes on tolerating everything for days together. He does not say anything but anger keeps building up inside him. There may be some little things that trouble him and annoy him every day, but he suppresses them. Then one day, when his suppressed anger reaches boiling point, he explodes with a big blast. He screams and insults and can even go to the extent of smashing whatever he can lay his hands on. This is the blaster pattern.

Blamer Pattern

People having this pattern always try to put the blame on others and furnish wonderful excuses. For every matter that goes wrong, they have a bank of ready excuses, such as: 'It was raining heavily today... There was a power cut for two hours... I had to entertain unexpected guests...' In this way they constantly blame somebody or something for their inability to complete their work.

Such people never feel responsible for themselves. Someone else is always there to be blamed for their suffering. They even feel that the reason why they could not achieve success in life was the behaviour of their father, mother or superiors at the workplace. This is what is called as the blamer pattern.

Breaker Pattern

Some people do make a start but cannot finish the job at hand. They develop a pattern of leaving things incomplete. This prevents them from learning new things; they are always busy with trying to complete their old unfinished tasks. Every now and then, their work comes to a standstill.

Miser Pattern

Some people are afflicted with the miser pattern. It is not just related to money; it encompasses and adversely affects the development of all aspects of an individual's life—physical, mental, emotional, social, financial and spiritual. People having this pattern are stingy in every matter, big or small. They are miserly even while laughing. If you tell them a cracking joke, they don't laugh. If they do, they laugh in instalments or go home and laugh. It is for these kinds of people that laughter clubs have come up. Since they cannot laugh heartily, somebody forcefully brings them to the club and makes them laugh out loud. It is then that they open up a bit and feel relaxed.

Counter Pattern

A person having the counter pattern counts only the negative things in his life. If he has 31 teeth in strong and healthy condition, he doesn't notice them; instead his tongue always reaches out for that one missing tooth. Such a person repeatedly observes only the things that are missing in his life. When he visits a garden, he first looks at the thorns and then at the flowers. As his attention is caught up in the thorns first, the flowers no longer look like flowers to him. If you marvel at the beauty of flowers first, the thorns won't bother you much. When you first look at the positives, the negatives won't concern you much.

Doubter Pattern

Victims of this pattern cast a doubt on everything. When sorrow appears in their life, they believe that this sad state of theirs would continue forever. They believe that happiness is temporary and sorrow permanent. They always doubt happiness thinking, 'Is it real? Is it going to last?'

Once you begin to know yourself, your real self, you will realize that you are happiness; your very existence is happiness. Happiness is permanent. You shall then never doubt it again. You therefore need to develop a habit: When happiness arrives, do not doubt it. When sorrow appears, certainly doubt it. Say to yourself, 'This sorrow has come only to go away.'

Whenever somebody criticizes a third person, you never doubt him. You feel the person being criticized must be bad. But if someone were to praise somebody, you doubt whether the person being praised is indeed so good. The mind has got habituated to this pattern.

Later Pattern

Those who have the later pattern simply postpone everything. They put off everything to the last moment. This procrastination could be due to a number of beliefs including wanting to be perfect or a false sense of security that things will take care of themselves. Because of this pattern, such people are constantly in stress. Some people do make a start but cannot finish the job at hand.

Never Pattern

Those who have the later pattern begin late. Those who have the breaker pattern begin but give up midway. Those who have the never pattern never begin at all. In other words, the never pattern signifies laziness. This pattern could be caused by fear or lethargy. But in any case these people have made up their minds that for some tasks there is no point even in trying.

Breaking Patterns

All patterns need to be broken. As long as these patterns exist inside you, you cannot open up and blossom; success will be out of reach.

Patterns signify wrong habits and tendencies that drive you away from your true nature—which is love, happiness and success. Every person has some wrong habit or the other. If you don't work on removing these habits, they deepen and develop into rigid patterns.

> *There is a man who has no control over his anger. He keeps picking fights with everyone. At home he unnecessarily shouts at his wife and children. This spoils the homely atmosphere and leads to constant clashes. This man never comes to realize that his anger has turned into a deep-rooted pattern. Influenced by his pattern, even his children start getting angry over petty matters. His wife as well develops this habit of throwing fits of rage at her*

children and neighbours. Thus the flames of fury burn not only him but also his family. This pattern sows only negative seeds in his life and that of others. He definitely suffers a major loss in the future.

Don't you feel that it is of utmost importance to work on eradicating such patterns before all your relations turn sour and you and your family fall into the endless pit of failure? If you are able to understand the implications of such patterns, apply the three steps outlined below to break them and experience the happiness of a liberated life.

Step One: Identify

The first thing you need to do to break patterns is to identify all the patterns you have. There are three ways to identify patterns. The first way is to observe yourself and contemplate. You will identify your patterns while passing through certain situations, or while working together with people, or while maintaining your relationships.

When you discover the patterns of your body and mind, write them down in your diary. All your patterns will come to light once you start thinking on them. Before you begin to contemplate you might believe that you don't have many patterns. For instance, you might think that you have only a little bit of the fire pattern and nothing else. But on serious reflection you will realize that you may be having some other patterns too out of the main ones such as the fear pattern, liar pattern, blamer pattern, blaster pattern (exploding of emotions), later pattern (procrastination), never pattern (laziness), counter pattern (always counting your sorrows and others' joys), miser pattern, etc. Once all your patterns come to light, you can start working on them. Building castles in the air is not going to break these patterns. Solid steps are needed for solid missions. When you realize what your patterns are through contemplation, write them down on a piece of paper and burn it off with full faith that you are getting rid of these patterns.

The second way to identify your patterns is to let others inform you of them. Take the help of your friends and family. Ask them what are the patterns that they can see in you. If they love you, they will certainly give you a correct feedback telling you all about the patterns they find in you. In this way, you shall be able to identify even the subtlest of patterns. Subtle patterns are those bad habits which we cannot notice ourselves, but they are visible to our friends and well-wishers. For example, a friend may tell you, 'You get angry too much... You delay every task... You lie... You consider your suffering to be more than others' suffering... You never consider others' feelings...' With this honest feedback from your friend, you wake up to the fact that you have many patterns. All along you were unaware of these patterns inside you. Your friend's frank opinion brought all your patterns to light.

In this manner you can ask for help in identifying your patterns. Your patterns harm everyone, but most of all they harm you. The fire pattern causes hypertension, headache, hair loss and also spoils your relations with your family, friends and colleagues at work. This is the root cause of failure.

The third way to spot your patterns is to read spiritual and self-help books. Like you are reading this book at present. As you become aware of your patterns, you will realize for the first time that there are also some unidentified patterns in you which need to be brought out and scrutinized. Contemplation, fine intellect and concentration of mind help in bringing forth the hidden patterns too.

Do not bring home rubbish under the excuse of reading something. Protect your brain from such news stories, magazines, books and advertisements that drain out its energy and its health. Now let us learn the second step of the formula to break patterns.

Step Two: Understand

In the first step of the formula, you learnt to identify your patterns. Now in the second step, you need to understand them. There is a difference between identifying your patterns and understanding them. When you come to know that you have the fire pattern, you have only identified it, not understood it. You just looked at it unconsciously and then forgot about it. Your fits of temper still go on. This means that this pattern has only come to light.

When a pattern surfaces time and again, you then have to look at it consciously and with full awareness. If an infuriating incident occurs and you get angry, you can identify that your fire pattern is at work. Now at the second step, you have to look at this anger from every aspect and observe the exact effects it has on your body and mind. Pay attention to and ponder on what exactly happened before the incident, during the incident and after the incident. You will begin to understand your fire pattern. Recall all the losses you have suffered till date due to anger. If this pattern is getting rigid by the day, think of all the problems that may crop up and trouble you in the future. Recall your state before and after you got angry. Meditate and mull over all these facets. Hereafter, whenever you get angry, you will know in advance what that angry state is like and what are its results. The second step of 'understanding your pattern' is complete here. Now you can say that you have understood your pattern. Thus you see that there is a lot of difference between identifying a pattern and understanding it. The action of understanding takes place with awareness. When you have understood your pattern, your chances for inner transformation go up.

> *There is a very fat man. His friends, family and well-wishers tell him, 'You have put on a lot of weight. You definitely need to exercise. Join a gym or get up early and go for a brisk walk. Or at least do some breathing exercises at home.' This man listens but takes no action. He is very lethargic by nature. Every day he keeps postponing his plans to begin exercising to the next day or next week. His friends have taken the first step for him. They have made him identify his patterns of laziness and procrastination. They have even warned him saying, 'Look, if you don't exercise, you will suffer from high or low blood pressure, heart problems, knee pain or a myriad of other ailments.' Yet this man does not budge. He is himself aware that he needs to exercise but sadly he is a slave of his habits. One day, he suddenly gets a heart attack. The doctor tells him, 'If you don't start exercising hereafter, you might die.' Now he gets a jolt and starts exercising after his recovery.*

If a pattern comes to light again and again, and yet you don't do anything about it or learn anything from it, then life gives you a jolt to wake you up. Nature keeps sending messages to you to help improve your understanding.

Choose any one of your patterns. Look at all its different forms. Bring before your eyes all the events and ill-effects of this pattern that have occurred in your life till date. Supposing you have the 'disorganized pattern'. It is your habit to keep things in disarray. Now look at all the problems that it has caused. You never find the thing you want, especially when you are in a hurry. For example, if somebody in your family accidentally burns his hand and you just cannot find the ointment quickly. This leads to unwarranted pain and damage, which you would never want. Sometimes you may be locked out due to misplaced keys and face a lot of trouble. At other times you simply fail to find the required file at office... you know the rest.

Taking another example, let us suppose that you have the latecomer pattern. You are always late. Now find out what all aspects of your life are being adversely affected by this pattern. Consider what are the losses that you are incurring and how it is hampering your progress due to being late for all your activities from morning to night. If your meeting is scheduled at 7:00, you reach at 7:30 and embarrass yourself in front of all your colleagues and bosses. Your image suffers. You lose more time in finding out the points discussed during that missed half hour. All you get is piecemeal information. This causes a delay in your decision which was supposed to be based on this information. This affects the company's progress too. You may get a reprimand or be furnished a memo. Thus you pay dearly for that half-hour delay for a long duration.

Supposing you wake up late in the morning in spite of deciding to rise early. This has a cumulative effect on your entire day's schedule. If your office hours begin at 10:00, you reach there at 10:30. This has a negative impact on your record. This habit gradually goes on to develop into a deep-rooted tendency and you begin to do everything late in life.

If you think that the latecomer pattern does not cause major harm, read on. This pattern, and for that matter, any pattern takes a severe toll on all spheres of your life—physical, mental, social, financial and spiritual. At the physical level, you get up late, you do not exercise and your health suffers. At the mental level, your work is recognized late. You understand the requirements of your project late. You even understand jokes late. This pattern causes mental stress and uneasiness. You need to run about at the last moment to complete things. It affects you financially. You get a job late, you start earning late. You get a promotion late. If your money gets blocked up somewhere, you receive it late too. At the social level, you reach parties or functions late and displease people. When this goes on time after time, you create a bad impression and your dignity goes down. This pattern also affects you spiritually. Since you get everything late, you get wisdom late too. You take a long time to understand the knowledge being imparted to you. Unfortunately you also receive grace late.

If someone has this pattern right from childhood, he crosses every phase of life late. His studies take a long time to complete, he gets a job late, he marries late, he begets children late and receives happiness of life late. One pattern can cause so much mayhem. Visualize the impact of all your patterns on the whole of your life. You shall then understand them. Without understanding your patterns, it is very difficult to liberate yourself from them.

You know that you have some wrong habits. You also know that you shall attain success very soon if you give up those habits. Then why don't you give them up? This is one of the biggest questions of life. Some people do want to give them up but simply cannot; they are helpless. As the saying goes: 'First man makes habits and then habits make man.' But the good news is that you can break all your patterns. The time to break all your habits and patterns has now arrived.

One way to understand your pattern deeply is to tell about it to yourself or a family member in your own words. It is essential that you confess all the difficulties you went through because of the pattern, how much you had to lie, how much you had to deceive and how much you had to suffer. In this way, you complete the second step of understanding your pattern.

It is possible that after identifying and understanding your pattern, a sense of guilt may crop up in your mind. Do not allow this to happen. Guilty conscience delays the process of coming out of the pattern. Hence, at the very outset, accept your pattern with love, which is the third step. Only when you are able to accept your pattern can you honestly begin your efforts to come out of it. The third and final step to break patterns is explained next.

Step Three: Transcend

The third step to break your patterns is to simply give them up for love. When you love yourself and your family, then it is this love that stirs you to break your patterns. Only love can make this happen. The very basis of life is love. Love is complete in itself.

If you love yourself, never lie to yourself. Never hide anything from yourself. If not with anybody else, at least be honest with yourself. Tell yourself the truth and everything about you without any deceit. As soon as you do this, you will get freedom from a lot of false beliefs, wrong habits and problems.

If you are trying to make your body a temple to achieve complete success, throw out all the garbage of bad habits and patterns from this temple, because you love God. If you feel that you are working for your own personal self, suffering will remain. Fear of success and failure will remain. When all your work is for God, the power of love makes it easy. If true love and devotion for God has awakened in you, you can break any pattern with great ease.

Finally, give yourself this auto-suggestion: 'I am breaking free from this pattern. God Himself is helping me out. God wants me to be free as quickly as possible. With His help, I am achieving complete freedom from this pattern.' Love and faith in God liberates us from patterns, wrong tendencies and wrong attractions.

You can also apply Truth Thinking Technique described in the previous chapter whenever the pattern raises its head. So whenever you feel the urge for anger, say to yourself 'Thank you for peace' and desist from the pattern.

Liberate yourself from every adversary of complete success and every pattern by using this magical three-step formula of identifying, understanding and transcending.

◆◆◆

Practical Exercise

List down the key patterns that are obstacles in your life. Identify the pattern in Step 1. Write down the negative impact of the pattern in the physical, mental, social, financial and spiritual areas of your life to understand the pattern better. Write down how the pattern has impacted your past, its influence on your present and its possible impact on your future. Then lovingly (without resistance) give up the pattern.

What next?

Since fear is a major pattern which is present in most people in one form or the other, let us understand it in further detail in the next chapter. You shall find some additional insights as well as techniques to conquer patterns besides the 3-step formula discussed in the current chapter.

16
Conquering Fear

The pattern of fear is a major hurdle on the path of complete success. It does not let you open up and blossom in life. It holds you back from tapping the innate powers hidden inside you. Any amount of progress you make will always be incomplete if you have fears. Never live like a coward and never heed to the advice given by cowards. Let people say whatever they want to, but you should never hesitate to experiment and explore your way through.

There are some people who are always scared and weak. Such people do nothing but prophesize the end of the world. Every new task that needs to be done arouses the fear of failure in their hearts. When you were little, you did as much as a hundred and fifty new experiments a day, but now you have forgotten that art. You need to revive that quality of courage. Make yourself a fearless being and walk hand-in-hand with courage. Courage is the essential factor that will take you towards success.

Do a self-check by asking yourself these questions: How much do I fear what people think about me? How much of courage do I have to try out something new? How much will I lose by living a fear-ridden life? What are the things I shall gain if I live fearlessly?

The moment you find answers to these questions, the courage to take an initiative will awaken inside you. You will be able to take the first step towards success. Otherwise you will only fear drowning in the sea of life and being eaten by sharks of failure. You will fail even before you begin.

Art of looking at fear: 'in spite of'

When starting with something new, any human being will experience some amount of fear. It's normal. If you think that you shouldn't feel fear at all, you are imposing an unreasonable condition on yourself. Your mind should be made unconditional, and for this, remember the words: 'in spite of'. In spite of feeling scared, do the least that you can do in a given situation. If you are able to do just that much, even then you can reach the highest state of success. In every situation, do whatever is possible for you. Tell your mind, 'Whatever is possible for you, do only that much. In spite of fear, can you take two steps forward?' If your mind says 'yes', take those steps. And if it says 'no', consider it as a trick of the mind.

This is because fear is just a feedback. When you take up some new work, the fear that you feel lets you know that this work is something new. If your body has never done that kind of a job before, it gives you a feedback.

When a computer or robot does not have something in its memory, it pops up a message which is something like: 'This command cannot be recognized, no information can be provided.' Look at fear in the same fashion. You will be free of fear only when you do not impose the condition that fear shouldn't arise in you. If you impose this condition, you will always have the fear at the back of your mind that fear may arise. Stop fearing fear.

All successful people in the world have experienced fear before accomplishing their feats. But they persisted with their job in spite of fear and that is why they succeeded. You have to do exactly the same. In spite of fear, move ahead as much as is possible for you.

Nature has placed both necessary and unnecessary fears in man, which keep increasing and decreasing as per time and situation. The best way to liberate yourself from fear is to face fear head-on. Do the things that you fear doing. First prepare a list of the things you fear doing. Then, one by one, start doing them. These may be: speaking on stage, completing work before time, playing with a dog, talking to a stranger, standing at heights, asking questions to your teacher, attending a funeral, etc. Begin your experiment.

Apart from encountering your fears, recall and list down all those activities that you have fruitfully accomplished in the past. You must have experienced the fulfilling sense of success on their accomplishment. By reliving those experiences, you can boost up your self-confidence. This confidence will inspire you to accept challenging tasks. With regular practice, there will be a significant growth in your courage, confidence and determination.

Consistent practice and courageously carrying out challenging tasks is the only way to liberate yourself from fear and hesitation. If you manage to convince yourself to willingly do things that are possible, you can certainly do them no matter how tough they are. Conversely, if you are not ready to do even the easiest of things, it will be impossible for you to work on challenging tasks.

When you face fear head-on, you will realize that fear did not exist at all! Whenever fear knocks at the door of your mind, don't open it yourself; let your self-confidence open it for you. When confidence opens the door, there will be nobody outside. Fear cannot exist in the presence of confidence. Fear and confidence are antipodes—like darkness and light. When you put the light on, darkness disappears.

Thus the first thing you should do is to stop fearing fear and make friends with it. Accept the fact that you have fear. If for some reason you feel some amount of fear, make use of that reason to your advantage. For example, if students study harder due to fear of failing in their exams, this fear is useful! But if fear is turning into a mental illness, cure it by giving yourself these auto-suggestions:

- I am courageous. I have stopped fearing fear. I'm friends with my fear.
- I can remain balanced and thereby complete every task successfully.
- Good and courageous people are entering my life.
- Every day, in every way, my mind and body are getting better and better.
- The limitless power of God is guiding me in every way from all directions.
- The adversity that does not kill me makes me stronger.

Repeated self-suggestions will generate fearlessness in you. Self-suggestions make it possible to attain holistic health, build a powerful character, enhance self-esteem, and achieve courage and complete success.

A courageous person does not die every day out of fear; he dies only once. Take a pledge not to die before your death. Majority of people live a life ridden with fears—it is as good as dying every day of their life. But don't fear death so much that it stops you from living your life.

If you want to achieve anything substantial in life, stop fearing failure. Your fears block your way to success. Do not stop trying for fear of failure. You become a failure when you stop trying. You are not a failure until you stop trying.

People who seek a safe haven for themselves can never achieve big. Brave people will tell you, 'If you are scared of taking a risk, take it immediately.' When you confront fear with this sort of courage, you will realize that fear never existed at all.

◆◆◆

Practical Exercise

As already mentioned, make a list of all your big and small fears. Subsequently start working on conquering each fear one by one using the wisdom and techniques described in the last two chapters.

What next?

There is a higher dimension of thinking which is called viveka. That's what we will learn in the next chapter.

17
Power of Viveka

The next power required for complete success is *viveka*. Viveka means the power to discriminate between the Truth and the untruth. Hence it is often referred to as discriminative intelligence. It is the power that helps you discern the right from the wrong. It is the power of a flexible intellect.

Viveka has been given to man to help him make right decisions by understanding the difference between the right and wrong, the Truth and untruth. Inspect yourself in every situation: Are you able to see the Truth with clarity? When you learn to wield the sword of viveka, you will swish aside the untruth and have a clear view of the cause of sorrow, the path to happiness and the summit of success. Since reflection with viveka has nowadays become a rarity among people, they cannot make out the difference between diamonds and coals. Without contemplation, even diamonds of wisdom are mere bits of coal. When you sharpen your sword of viveka, you will be able to judge which knowledge is like a philosopher's stone against the knowledge which is like an ordinary stone lying on the roadside. You will know which one to retain and which one to discard.

Viveka is a blessing endowed upon every human being. Those who make use of it are the ones who always remain happy. Happiness is already present within us; it needn't be brought from outside. It is only because of losing the habit of viveka-filled contemplation that man lives an aimless, unsuccessful life.

How to wield the sword of viveka

If you see someone at a carnival wandering about with a long face, what will you do? Won't you remind him that he is at a carnival? He is supposed to enjoy it! If he has been entrusted with the care of a child by someone for some time, he loses his viveka at once because of the obligation. Same is the case if someone gives him a bag to carry. He forgets that he has come to the carnival for recreation. All his attention is on the baggage. He keeps lamenting, 'Why me…? Is this what I have come here for…? Why do I have to suffer all this…?' This person needs to be reminded that even though a bag is hung on his shoulder or there is a baby in his arms, he is still in a carnival. He shouldn't forget that a carnival is meant for fun and joy.

This world is a carnival. We have been sent to earth to derive happiness. The human body is the child that we are carrying around at the carnival, and there is a purpose behind this. We have come to earth with this body to achieve the ultimate purpose of human life. But we have totally forgotten all about it. All we see is the difficulties associated with the body and the burdensome baggage of responsibilities. The slightest pain that our body experiences makes us grumble, 'Why me? Why this pain…?' We identify ourself with our body and lose our viveka. We only need to remember where we are and what we are doing. We have to enjoy this carnival in spite of physical difficulties, i.e. we have to fulfil the purpose of coming to earth. Otherwise all the while we tend to focus on pain and suffering. Even on getting a human birth, our face shows no trace of joy or wonder, because we have forgotten the art of contemplation. Our viveka is almost listless.

Everyone has been given the sword of viveka. Everyone is graced with intellect. But it is not being used and thereby getting rusty over the years. It once again needs to be polished. It once again needs to be sharpened, so that as soon as thoughts of joy and sorrow appear, you can slice them into two categories: thoughts of Truth and thoughts of untruth. You can differentiate between thoughts rooted in ignorance and those arising from wisdom.

For an ignorance-filled thought such as 'I am very disturbed', viveka will at once prompt you, 'Are you disturbed or are you allowing yourself to be disturbed?' For a thought like 'I am getting bored', viveka will ask you, 'Are you getting bored or are you letting yourself get bored? What exactly does *getting bored* mean?' You will be pleasantly surprised at the results when you start brandishing the sword with skill. Viveka will awaken you to the fact that it is you who let yourself get bored or disturbed. Should you really allow that to happen? You will get a firm 'no' as the answer and those thoughts will vanish.

The thought 'My colleague is troubling me' will instantly be replaced with 'He is troubling me because I am giving him a chance to trouble me.' Ask yourself, 'Should I give him this chance?' Viveka will reply, 'No!' Then whatever that person does, he will simply not be able to trouble you at all. Your distress will evaporate in an instant. This is what viveka-filled contemplation can do. It will ensure that positive thoughts always prevail over the negative.

Viveka goes to sleep when the mind is reigned by unconsciousness and ignorance. This gives a free entry to incidents and circumstances to trouble you. With consciousness as your gatekeeper, no person, thought, event, dealing or weather can bother you. If the level of awareness rises within us due to viveka, it means that the power of viveka has started working in our lives.

Apart from discerning the right from the wrong, viveka can also help us understand the difference between the real 'I' and the false 'I'. We will realize that we are not the body; we merely use it. Our body is not our existence; we are separate from the body. We use our body. How can we be the thing that we use? When we say 'my body, my mind, my intellect and my soul', the 'me' has to be something else. It is due to viveka that the question arises in your mind: 'Who am I actually?' Without viveka, one cannot even begin to think on these lines. You cannot get even a little bit close to the real 'I'; you will be miles away. When you say, 'There is a soul inside me', then the viveka asks you, 'If there is a soul inside you, then who are *you*? In whom is there a soul? Your body, mind, intellect and also your soul are distinct from you; then who is the one talking within you?' Thus with the sword of viveka a new consciousness awakens within you.

When you wield the sword of viveka in every incident and situation, you will question yourself: 'Who is the one getting worried? Who is the one who wants success? Who am I?' A new perspective will unfold. With reflection, you will understand the reality about exactly what happens during moments of fear, sadness, anger, boredom, hatred, etc. and with whom it happens. With this new outlook, the feeling of wonder and of being the non-doer will go on rising.

> *A boy was playing chess with his father. When he was attacked by the queen, bishops and rooks, he got scared. His thoughts ran amok. 'What's going to happen next? Will I be able to save myself?' These thoughts left him anxious and nervous. And then suddenly he remembered that he was playing with his father, and not the queen, bishops and rooks! All his anxiety vanished. The moment he realized the reality, all his problems dissolved at once. Thereafter even if he was attacked by all the chess pieces, he played with a relaxed frame of mind. He understood that his father was making his move with the queen to teach him the skills of the game. Hence he was supposed to learn the game and not get frightened by the queen.*

In the same manner, we must realize the Truth of life. Whom are we dealing with in life? With whom are we playing this game of life? With our father—the ever-loving God. If you are able to recall this Truth in all circumstances, a great transformation will occur in your life. Henceforth whenever you are attacked by fear, worry, stress, sorrow or anger, you will ply the sword of viveka and remind yourself, 'With whom exactly is this happening? Who am I? Who am I playing with and for what?'

Imagine that you are standing by the riverside and your reflection is seen in the water. With every ripple in the water, your reflection wavers. Looking at this, if someone offers you his sympathy by saying 'Oh, your reflection is trembling!', you will tell him, 'It's only my reflection that is trembling, not me! It makes no difference to me. Whatever is happening, is happening with my reflection.' Likewise, when you understand the Truth of life, you will realize that whatever is happening in your life is happening with your body, mind or intellect; and not with you. You are separate from these entities. The moment you understand this, you will easily free yourself from every sorrow, every worry, every anxiety.

When you are given some object to use, you merely use it; you don't become that object. For instance, if you are given the microphone to speak through it, you do not become the microphone. If you use a car, you are not the car. In the same way, you merely use your body, you are not the body.

Man's biggest false belief is that he thinks he is the body. When you liberate yourself from this belief and know experientially that you are not the body, your life will take a U-turn. You will feel so alive, vibrant and energetic that you will never need any external stimulation to keep you happy. You won't require any reason to be happy. Your existence would be enough and complete in itself for you to be happy.

With the awakening of viveka, you will realize that happiness has already been arranged for—right within you, right from the beginning. You have only forgotten how to experience that good feeling (of being alive), which you are feeling right now. It is time that someone told you that the life, the happiness that you are seeking outside is right inside you. If you can comprehend this Truth, you will start getting immense joy from within you. You will never feel the need to indulge in fights and arguments in order to feel alive. (External stimulations like those only make you lose your viveka.) Then a new dimension of your life will open, only after attaining which you can be called a complete person.

The five secrets of true success—the power of thoughts, words, faith, intention and viveka—have been revealed in this book. Use these powers to defeat failure. Positive feelings, thoughts and words are the backbone of success. And the power of viveka and character are essential to maintain success. Else, people do attain success only to lose it soon. Viveka helps you to remain successful always. With every successful endeavour, you gain in experience and self-confidence. And with every experience, it becomes much easier to achieve more success. Then you shall attain the understanding of the ultimate purpose of success; and your body will become a medium for the ultimate expression of God. This is the truest form of success.

With the knowledge of all the secrets of complete success, annihilate all your patterns, obstacles, vices, fears, failures and wrong habits. Herald your success and begin your work on the playground of life. Learn from each failure and beware of letting your ego inflate upon striking success. Implementation of this understanding will place you atop a new peak of success—where the search for success ends, where there is unprecedented success of having achieved the ultimate purpose of success.

❖❖❖

Practical Exercise

1. *Whenever you get any negative feeling, say anxiety, ask yourself, 'Am I feeling anxious? Or am I allowing myself to feel anxious?' Carry out this exercise with every negative feeling and observe the result.*
2. *Whenever anything happens with you, say pain/stress/dullness, ask yourself, 'Is this happening with me, or is it happening with my body /mind /intellect? Who am I?'*

What next?

Having explored the higher dimensions of thinking, let us now delve into the realm of feeling.

Part V

Success in the realm of feeling

Unlock the Natural Leader within you

18
Self Energizing for Leadership

What is it that differentiates leaders from others? A leader is one whose focus is on solution of problems, resolution of difficulties and answers to questions. He looks within himself for the cause of problems, and not outside. Never does he shirk his responsibility by putting blame on others. Nor does he blame destiny, misdeeds of previous births, circumstances or people. He has awakened and shunned the blame game.

One who is not a leader is someone who always blames his destiny. He consoles himself by saying that his failures are a result of wrong deeds committed in his previous births. As he never gives up blaming his fate or other people, he always remains unsuccessful.

Once success is achieved, a leader does not rest on his glory; he continues to explore further. There are two benefits of this: firstly, new possibilities can be sighted, and secondly, the danger of regressing is averted.

When you stop after achieving success and refrain from exploring new possibilities, there is every possibility of backsliding. As you stop, you get free time, during which you attract and entertain negative thoughts. Awareness drops and laziness attacks you during your free time. Hence you need to learn to spend your spare time with awareness. Meditation, creative work and planning your next progressive project will help you move ahead. Even if you don't make much progress, you will at least be saved from slipping backwards.

New opportunities open up only when we learn from our critics. If you fear being criticized, you cannot achieve Complete Success. A true leader does not feel upset by the criticism behind his back. In fact he analyzes what is being said about him and converts it into a stepping stone for his progress. He knows very well that no one ever kicks a dead animal. People criticize only the live and the thriving. He treats the criticism as information—gained free of charge!

On the other hand Mr. Unsuccessful gets depressed on hearing people talk bad about him behind his back. He gives those things more importance than they deserve, and stops working. Little does he know that such criticizers are all but disciplined. Saint Tukaram has in fact gone on to say that people who criticize us should stay next-door to us, so that we get to know our shortcomings as early as possible. On the other hand he has also advised us not to criticize others.

The reason a leader is focused on solutions is because he does not get carried away by his feelings and moods. He knows how to use feelings to always stay motivated.

Master your mood

If someone were to describe heaven to you in a dull and detached manner, you would be left thinking of hell instead. And if someone were to narrate about hell with enthusiasm and emphasis on the subject, you would think that it is heaven he is talking about! Enthusiasm is the lifeblood of success. The flame of enthusiasm instils life into the most boring of activities. A successful person infuses inspiration in his co-workers too. Motivated by one's zeal, a person aiming for complete success works in harmony with one and all, due to which his success is assured. All of you who aspire for success should grab onto this secret.

How does a successful person maintain his level of enthusiasm? He discovers at least one interesting aspect of each event and activity, which fills his cup of enthusiasm to the brim. This converts every snake into a ladder for him and every difficulty into a challenge.

An unsuccessful person is only able to look at the superficial aspect of every activity and soon his enthusiasm dies out. Therefore every problem becomes a snake for him and every challenge a difficulty. Snakes and difficulties invite failure. Hence always infuse your mind with thoughts of success, happiness and faith. Let your mind ponder over positive and inspiring thoughts for long durations. If you always want to be zealous, you will have to bring thoughts of courageous and rousing activities. If you happen to lose link with this practice, don't fret; again revise and understand the principles of thought and start afresh.

Life is about being lively; don't make it a living death. It is high time you started living life as it is meant to be. Live your life brimming with enthusiasm, filled with the courage of acceptance, and blooming with joy. Let thoughts of liveliness drive your life. They will bestow you with health, success as well as help you achieve the ultimate purpose of success.

By keeping your mood firmly under your grip through the power of thoughts, it is possible to create a state of mind which provides a continuous supply of enthusiasm and bliss. If you keep your body, mind and intellect inspired with regular inputs from positive thoughts and teachings of great personalities, you can bring about immeasurable growth in your happiness and work proficiency. Also keep inspiring spiritual books within your reach. As soon as you get some free time, start reading good, genuine books and outstanding autobiographies or biographies. By adopting this principle of reading-contemplation-implementation, you can always be composed, balanced and completely fulfilled.

If there were a mantra for boosting enthusiasm, it would definitely be: *Never wait for the right mood to set in; just start working and set your mood.* A successful person never waits to be in the 'mood' to start working. He knows that if you just start working, your mood automatically sets in for that work.

When you are 'not in the mood to work', speed up your actions. Walk swiftly, write quickly, dial the phone number speedily, bathe in no time, clean up your room in a flash, or rapidly move things from one place to the other. This tempo prevents your mind from becoming a slave of your mood. You are indeed unsuccessful if you are a slave of your mood. An unsuccessful person cannot start up the machine of his body-mind without the right mood; whereas a successful person can start up his body-mind whenever he wants to. He has the remote control of his body-mind in his own hands. With a single command, his body-mind mechanism begins to work.

An unsuccessful person hands over his remote control to others and simply forgets whom he gave it to. Every small thought can ruin his mood. So remember the mantra for boosting your enthusiasm: Master your mood.

◆◆◆

Practical Exercise

List down incidents that spoil your mood. Apply the method described in this chapter to master your mood.

What next?

Let us learn to get rid of the burdensome feelings of the past and the future in the ensuing chapter.

19
Live in the Present

There was once a severe famine in the kingdom of Emperor Asoka. The emperor let open the royal granary for the general public, so that none of his subjects would go without food. It was evening time and the light began to fade. The granary was being shut down for the day when an old man hobbled to the gates and asked for some wheat. The soldiers said, 'We are closing now; come back tomorrow.' But he was not ready to leave empty-handed. Just then, a youth came by and told the soldiers to give him the wheat. The soldiers agreed at once.

The old man took out a big sack and gave it to the soldiers. Looking at it, the soldiers said, 'You won't be able to lift so much grain!' But the old man insisted that he wanted an entire sackful. The soldiers filled it up and gave it to him. Indeed, he could not lift the heavy sack.

So the youth carried it on his shoulders and walked along with the old man. Suddenly a chariot came towards them and stopped. Some men dismounted and greeted the youth—who was none other than Emperor Asoka himself. The old man was shocked. 'The Emperor carried my burden!' He shuddered at this thought. He started mumbling his apologies but the emperor assured him, 'Don't worry. Come and sit in the chariot. I'll leave you home.'

The old man was hesitant and stuttered, 'No...no... How can I sit in your chariot!' On the emperor's insistence, he finally relented and climbed in. But he kept the sack of wheat on his head. The emperor said, 'Why don't you put it down?' The old man said, 'No, Your Majesty, how can I?! You are already carrying me in your chariot; I cannot be so selfish and add the burden of my sack as well.' The emperor exclaimed, 'What are you saying! You need not carry the burden; put it down. It does not make any difference to the chariot, whether you carry it on your head or put it down. The weight on the chariot will be the same.'

The old man may or may not have understood the point, but we should definitely understand it regarding our own burdens. The past and future are two heavy sacks that we carry on our head wherever we go. We constantly carry the baggage of what has happened and what all we have to do. Unload them onto the chariot of life. The life which is carrying you can carry your baggage as well.

If you get a question 'How will today be?', what will be your reply? If you have the right understanding, you will say, 'Today will be as I want it to be.' Otherwise it will be as your past wants it to be; you will live today as you lived yesterday.

For most people, the events of their past shape their future. The way they have been raised has created a mould in which they tend to live. They live their present in this mould, and if they do not break it, they live their future too in this mould. This implies that if the past has been sad, the future is also sad.

Some people look at the weather and make assumptions about their day. If the skies are dark and gloomy, they assume that their day would not go well, it would be dull and boring. Why do they get such thoughts just by looking at the dark clouds? It is because some unpleasant incidents have occurred in their past in the rainy weather. Some people dislike the monsoons. They feel depressed during that season. Why does this happen? There is a reason behind it. If they look back, they can recall that something disagreeable had happened in their lives in that season.

> *It was raining. A man was walking on the wet roadside when a passing car splashed mud on him. He was already anxious because he was getting late for work, and now to add to his woes, his clothes were spoiled. This incident created an impression in his mind that the rainy weather meant gloom. Henceforth whenever he saw dark clouds, his mind would recall only those feelings. Thus his past began to drive his present. And since we always receive proofs for the beliefs we harbour, our present shapes up exactly like the past, which corroborates our beliefs further. At the end of the day, he says, 'See, I knew that today would not be a good day.'*

A peacock dances when it sees the dark clouds, while some people feel down in the dumps! It happens because of the old programming of the mind. In order to get rid of it, you have to fill your mind with positive, optimistic thoughts. These thoughts are especially required when you are lost in the sea of misery and sorrow.

It is only after the darkest hour that a new day breaks out. Hence do not allow sorrow or depression to overwhelm you. If you remain sad and depressed for many years, you get habituated to it. You then become a burden to your family and yourself. At least for the sake of your near-and-dear ones and your profession, be optimistic. You have been blessed with a lot of good things and qualities by God, look at them.

When you become aware of all the good things you already have, your sadness can disappear. A new life, a new morning is when your awareness awakens. New Year does not begin on 1st January; it begins when you wake up to the present—the reality.

There are some people in the world who carry wrong notions about people having a particular hairdo or a turban. In the past they may have seen some of these kinds of people involved in misdeeds, and on that basis they generalize their assumptions for the whole community. They think that the whole community is bad. Their mind gets programmed in the wrong manner because of past incidents. If you are one amongst them, you need to erase the past record from your mind, so that you get a chance to enter and enjoy a new life—a 'present tense' life.

Your future should be built in the present. Check how you are living the present. How are you spending the current moments? Is your time being spent with complete understanding or is it in confusion?

Do not let the repentance of yesterday and the worries of tomorrow pollute your today. As you climb towards the summit of success, lessen your burdens by dropping the sacks of the past and future. Lay them to rest. This is because the past is not bad, it is dead. The future is only in your imagination. This means only the present is the reality. You cannot do anything about your past or your future; only the present is in your hands. And the fact is that your future is shaped by your present. Hence just concentrate on making your present the best. Practise the art of keeping your mind focused on the job at hand. When you take care of the present, the future will take care of itself.

❖ ❖ ❖

Practical Exercise

List down the negative feelings you have about your past as well as your future. Now drop this baggage and let it go by tearing the list and burning it in a fire. After that raise your hands towards the sky and say, 'I am free. I am free. I am freedom.'

What next?

Let us learn to convert our negative feelings into positive by using another powerful method described in the following chapter.

20
Power of Acceptance

The natural way to energize yourself and be focused as a leader is by harnessing the power of acceptance.

A successful person has the ability to accept every episode in life, positive or negative. This is not blind acceptance though; what makes a successful person stand apart is his wisdom behind this feeling of acceptance. With this wisdom, he stays at the summit of success all his life. With the power of acceptance, he converts every failure into a stepping stone towards success.

Acceptance can be of two types: 1) Acceptance with complete understanding, which transforms us and our attitude & 2) Acceptance due to helplessness; a reluctant acceptance. There is neither a feeling of acceptance nor understanding in the second type, and the person curses his fate throughout his life.

If you have the feeling of unacceptance in your mind, i.e. you are not able to accept some incident or failure, then stop and think whether you have any preconceived notion about what success or failure is. Are you looking at the failure through the lenses of some false belief? How should you be really looking at it?

If you are seeing failure with the wrong outlook, you will never be able to accept it. It is time you flipped your outlook.

It may be difficult in the beginning to accept things. But as your feeling becomes more and more positive, and you gain more understanding, soon you will be able to accept things as they are.

Effect of acceptance in the journey of life

Look at little children when you take them along on a train journey. When the train pushes them forward, they too bend forward and when it pushes them backwards, they too bend backwards. They simply go along with the jolts of the train. They do not offer any kind of resistance to those movements. However, in the case of grownups, when the train pushes them forward, they press themselves backwards and when it pushes them backwards, they force themselves forward. This is what they do throughout the journey of their life. They keep resisting and struggling all along. When grownups alight from the train after a long journey, they feel fatigued in spite of having done nothing at all. But the children immediately jump down and start running around at the station feeling as fresh and happy as ever.

Grownups wear themselves down by rejecting every tug and jolt in the whole journey. You must go through your journey of life with the feeling of acceptance.

In the journey of complete success, how are you dealing with failures? Are you looking at them as roadblocks? Or are you pausing and asking yourself, 'Okay, now that failure has appeared, can I accept it?' If your answer is 'Yes, I can accept it', you will instantly feel better. Then you will be able to think through the failure with clarity. Whatever you do next will turn out to be the best and you will resume your journey of complete success with new zeal.

While using this technique of acceptance, some people may have questions like: 'If everything is to be accepted, should we not improve upon our mistakes? Should we not attempt to succeed? And will I get success as soon as I accept things?'

Of course you have to put in efforts to achieve complete success, but with both your hands. When you don't accept failure, it's like one of your hands is tied up behind your back and you are trying to solve a problem with only one hand. This is foolishness. Common sense says that it is much easier to solve problems using both your hands. To convert failure into a ladder to success, you need to accept it first. As soon as you accept it, both your hands become free. If your mind asks 'why only me?', explain to it, 'I need to come out of this situation and hence I must accept it first.' This is the right approach.

You should neither take up wrong means to achieve success nor fear failure and stop working. Once you accept failure, there is a radical change in the way you tackle the problem; you do it powerfully, with an open mind and with great ease. If your first step is wrong, all the subsequent ones will be wrong. That is why you must learn the technique of acceptance before you begin your efforts for complete success.

The general feeling among common people is that accepting failure is as good as running away from the problem. Acceptance is not fleeing from a situation; it is flying over a situation. You will be able to fly, because the moment you accept, you liberate yourself from the grip of negative energy.

Also, acceptance does not imply that you should stop having any wishes or stop the journey of complete success. In fact the journey of complete success gives you a direction. If you fail to reach your planned milestones for some reason, then instead of abandoning your quest, you must accept the situation. As soon as you do, you are able to discover newer and innovative methods to reach your destination. This keeps alive your chances of attaining complete success.

How to accept?

The way to accept is through a simple question: 'Can I accept this?' In life we come across many unwanted situations that in turn lead to misery. Even trivial incidents force us to retreat in our shell and make us very unhappy. To come out of that unhappiness, ask yourself, 'Can I accept this?' 'This' implies that which is making you unhappy. For instance, some unfavourable incident has occurred, so just ask yourself, 'Can I accept this?' ('this' means that unfavourable incident).

'Can I accept this?' — this little mantra can work wonders. Whenever any situation arises, you will find that your answer will be 'yes' in 100% of the smaller incidents. It is only because you haven't asked yourself that you have become withdrawn and constricted. Now after repeating this mantra, you won't live a closed life anymore.

When you get the benefit of this mantra in smaller incidents, you will find that in 99% of the average occurrences also, your answer will be 'yes'. Examples of average or medium occurrences are a small accident or someone insulting you, in which case you flinch back instantly. At that moment ask yourself, 'He has insulted me; can I accept this?' You will see that in 99% of the cases, your answer will be 'yes'. Thereby you will be immediately liberated from that thought. After the answer 'yes', many of your problems will be solved. Just make a habit of asking yourself in every situation, 'Can I accept this?' It may so happen that something may go wrong as soon as you wake up in the morning, someone may do some mischief, or you may hear the blaring of loud music coming from your neighbouring room or house, or dogs may not stop barking at night. In any case, just ask yourself, 'Can I accept this?' And if you are able to accept it then you will say, 'Let it go on. If the dogs are barking, let them bark, I am accepting it.' With this acceptance, a feeling of relief will instantly flood through you.

It is possible that you may get a negative answer in some situation. In that case, give yourself some time, and after an interval, ask yourself the same question again. For instance, some incident has occurred and you are unable to understand it. You feel it is not acceptable and your answer is 'no'. Accept your 'no' for the time being. After some time, ask again, 'Can I accept it now?' You will find that after some time a positive answer will begin to emerge. This is likely in some instances. A positive answer may not appear immediately, but after a few minutes or a few hours, you will get the answer as 'yes'. You will feel relieved at once.

However, even after trying repeatedly, if your answer is still, 'No, I cannot accept this', in those instances you should accept your unacceptance as well. Let us understand this with some examples. If you feel, 'I cannot tolerate to see this man's face', then ask yourself, 'Can I accept my unacceptability?' If you are worried and that worry is constantly eating you, just ask yourself, 'Can I accept this worry?' Your answer will be, 'Alright, so I am worried. I can accept this.' In this way when you accept your unacceptability, something new is created. You will be amazed by the results of acceptance when you accept your unacceptance by saying, 'Ok, this is how I am. I have faults but this is fine with me. I accept this.' A person who is black or white or short or fat is unable to accept himself. One says, 'I have ugly teeth, I cannot accept this.' But with this mantra he will say, 'Alright, I can accept my unacceptance.'

Let us look one more time at what you can do when you cannot accept something:

1. Try to accept the situation after some time.
2. Accept only some part of the situation. Accept bit by bit.
3. Accept only the negative feeling that the situation is causing by identifying the feeling.
4. Accept not being able to accept it. This is a very critical step. Ask yourself, 'Can I accept my unacceptance?'

How does acceptance work?

One of the laws of life is what is true at one level is true at all levels. As in small, so in big. As in the microcosm, so in the macrocosm. When you answer 'yes' to the 'Can I accept this?' question, then you have released your negative feelings associated with it. You may think that it is just a small step. But the fact is that it causes a giant shift in your consciousness. At that very moment, a lot of related and similar issues too get automatically accepted by your mind. As a result you begin to attract more positive things towards you. The moment you let go of a negative feeling through acceptance, you are telling your subconscious mind: 'I am open to the goodness and abundance of the universe. I am not going to cringe like a miser.' Then the law, *'What you focus on in your life is what multiplies in your life'*, takes over. The smallest letting go action helps you in every facet of your life. Not only do you become mentally free, but it affects you at the physical, emotional, social, financial and spiritual levels and sets off a chain reaction that reverberates through your entire being, taking you to quite a different place than you were before.

How do you use this knowledge that even a small act of acceptance causes a giant shift in your consciousness? Simple. Whenever you find yourself troubled by a huge problem, accept something small—either related to the problem or not. This small shift will help you tackle the bigger one too.

❖❖❖

Practical Exercise

List down incidents or situations that make you unhappy. Accept them one by one using the methodology described above.

What next?

Having accepted, the question now is, how do you know whether you have accepted? In chemistry, a litmus test is used to decide whether a given solution is acidic or not. Blue litmus is a special type of filter paper that turns red under acidic conditions. It is a test to see if the chemical reaction intended was successful and whether acid was produced or not. Similarly, is there some test that tells you whether your acceptance was successful or not? There is. When you have accepted it, the same problem or situation appears fresh and somehow seems different. So, how do you apply the litmus test? All you have to do is to review the situation once more in your mind. See the problem again. If your acceptance has worked—it usually does—then the problem or situation seems lighter and clearer. If there is still some negative emotion left, accept again by asking, 'Can I accept this?' See the situation yet again in your mind. Has it lightened? Keep doing so till you are fully clear.

You need to transcend past failures too. If you have truly accepted failure, it will remain only as a learning in your mind and not carry a baggage of emotions with it. Let us see what more can be done to overcome failure in the subsequent chapter.

21
Overcoming Failure

Failures appear in your life only for you to recreate and reinforce your desires. When you face setbacks in pursuit of your desire, it instils some more passion in you. You think to yourself, 'No, this is not done! I simply have to succeed now at all costs.' Unless there is zeal in your desire, you drag along saying, 'Oh, what's the hurry? Everything is going to happen... Success is on the way.' But when failure hits you, you wake up with a jolt and get the required fillip to show that 'I can do it'.

Whatever negative is happening with you is only for you to rekindle the desire to progress ahead. Failure too is preparation for complete success. Nature is forever providing you guidance; decode the messages that you receive and keep moving ahead. To move ahead, look at every event and failure with an eye of understanding.

When you start working on a new activity, keep your eyes and ears wide open. Be more alert. Life is continuously sending you messages to teach you and guide you for relentless growth. Develop an eye to discern and interpret these messages. If you work on the right message at the right time, you will achieve astonishing success.

How to look at failures

While working and experimenting with new activities, you may face numerous failures. Instead of getting disheartened in such situations, remind yourself that you do not have to fear failures. Just remember the example of a rubber ball. When a rubber ball falls to the ground, it bounces back immediately. In the same manner, when you find yourself in a difficult situation, you have to face it like a rubber ball. Take a lesson or two from the situation and be prepared for the next time. When you are able to do this, you will have learnt to leap forward in the right manner.

The more we heat gold, the more lustre it attains. Likewise, the more difficulties you face in life, the more you grow and shine. If you have changed your attitude with the right understanding, you can turn every failure into a stepping stone for success. This is because difficulties and obstacles help in awakening your hidden powers. Failures strengthen your desire for progress. Get rid of the misunderstanding that 'failures make me insecure and unsuccessful'.

Fear of failure

Ignorance about failure creates the feeling of insecurity. Most people are ignorant of the significance of failure. Even at the doorstep of success, they are plagued by apprehensive inner dialogue such as: 'What if I don't succeed in this project...? I don't want to fail... How will I face people if I fail...?' And it is these ignorant thoughts that often bring them failure. Hence at such times you have to assertively repeat only one thought to yourself: 'Moving ahead is safe for me. God wants me to move ahead.'

Most of the times you know that you must advance in your journey but you fear that there might be danger ahead. This puts you in a predicament. You are caught in a dilemma at the same time: joy of success and fear of failure. To help you decide which way to go, you have to give yourself the auto-suggestion mentioned earlier, which is: 'Moving ahead is safe for me. God wants me to move ahead.'

Do not leave your work unfinished out of the fear of failure. Complete every task you undertake. With positive thoughts you gain a new outlook and your self-confidence takes an upward turn. A successful man never entertains negative thoughts; only positive and Truthful thoughts fill his mind. With this outlook you can find a way even in failure. Failure is not unsafe; it is safe.

Everyone experiences the fear of failure while trying out some new and challenging experiments. But this fear should not stop you from learning and experimenting with the new. In any experiment, whether successful or not, the most important thing is learning. If you abandon your experiments fearing failure, how will you ever learn? An 'experiment' means a creative action meant for solving the problems you come across in life. Every incident that you encounter is meant to teach you a lesson of life. It is your need to learn the lessons that both the positive and negative incidents teach you, without getting entangled in the incidents themselves. When you go through these experiences, you will emerge a better person.

If you have faced failure in everything you have done till date, it does not imply that you will face failure in the future too. If at all you have this misconception in your mind, erase it. With time your level of mental maturity goes on increasing. Learn as much as you can from every incident. But don't compare yourself with others. A squirrel will learn only as much as it can. And an elephant will learn as much as it can. You must learn to the maximum of your capacity. Compare only with yourself and move ahead. If you march ahead towards complete success through ever new experiments, success will always be there by your side.

You need to know how things function. Let us understand this through an example. Supposing you are in an enemy jail. To escape from it, you must first thoroughly examine each and every corner of the jail, only then will you be able to decide whether it is easy or difficult to get out.

Gradually you will grasp the state of affairs in the jail. You might then realize that only a little effort is required for you to escape from it. The task that seemed tough in the beginning now looks quite simple after you gained understanding. Once you take stock of the situation in the jail, you will find a way out and escape easily. The gist is, for a person to be successful, it is important for him to gather knowledge about a few things beforehand. Having the right information at the right time helps.

If you do not have complete knowledge of the job at hand, you will certainly find it difficult. To bring any kind of work to its rightful conclusion, you need to understand it in all its entirety. It is imperative to be well-informed of the domain of work in which you want to excel. Remember that ignorance is the root cause of failure.

People have the attitude that 'the work that does not yield me any profit is futile'. The truth is that nothing goes in vain. No activity done by you, whether successfully or unsuccessfully, goes to waste. Whatever you do, it adds up to your experience, and in the process you are getting trained. During this period you actually undergo preparation for achieving the ultimate purpose of complete success.

Look at failure from a scientific perspective

When you do not succeed in your work, change your approach to this work and see what happens. Doing old jobs in a new manner can even lead to new inventions. By trying out all the possible methods, you will at least be able to discover the best method to do it. One way to accelerate the process of learning a new task is to visualize yourself doing the entire task from start to finish. Think it through. Whatever you want to gain expertise in, first do it in your mind. For instance, if you are a novice in using computers and want to become an expert in it, visualize yourself working on some program. See yourself hitting the appropriate keys for the function you want and clicking all the right tabs with the mouse. Do it in your mind exactly as you would in reality. When you start doing this, you will find yourself learning much quicker than others. Make best use of your spare time in this manner. With this method, you can learn anything within a short period—like playing cricket or chess, public speaking skills, driving a car, swimming, etc.

The time that you get to be by yourself is precious. Use it for self-development and for creating something new. Whenever you think, think only positive. Think of success; never ever think of failure. When caught up in difficulties, just believe that victory will be yours.

If you really want to succeed, you have to keep trying till your last breath. Edison faced failure after failure in his attempt to invent the electric bulb. This did not stop him from conducting hundreds of experiments. He relentlessly kept on trying until one day he finally succeeded. Even today Edison is known all over the world. Just like him, learn to keep a positive attitude towards failures.

When Edison was asked about how he could succeed after so many unsuccessful attempts, he said, 'After performing so many experiments, I found out which is the one formula for making the bulb. But along with it, I also learned of hundreds of such procedures that do not make the bulb. *Knowing what to do* is success, similarly *knowing what not to do* is also success.' Edison's attitude towards failures was such that they never made him unhappy.

Win every time, because the impossible is possible

The mantra for overcoming failure is: 'Win every time!' You will never be a victim of failure if you take care of one thing—Never let defeat defeat you. If you don't lose to defeat, you will always win! If you carry the fear of failure and you lose, you let failure create a place for itself in your mind. And it is this mistake that actually makes you fail. Otherwise, unless you lose in your mind, your defeat is never a defeat. When mountaineers are asked about their secret to success and how they could conquer the toughest of peaks, they invariably say, 'Before winning over the mountains, we first win over ourselves', which implies that a person's victory or defeat is decided in his own mind.

Losing is never defeat in itself; losing against defeat is defeat. You are defeated when you lose courage after losing. There are many people in this world who are scared of losing, and this makes them losers forever. The thoughts of losing make them lose. You should not get defeated by defeat. You are actually defeated by the thoughts of hopelessness that enter your mind upon defeat. Your failure is no more a failure if you persist with your efforts relentlessly; this failure is in fact a motivation for you to succeed. Take this motivation and march ahead.

Remember the mantra of complete success: *'I will always win because I no longer let defeat defeat me.'* Don't be put off by failure; use it as a stepping stone to march towards success.

Successful people will tell you that they too had to face numerous failures in life, but they always held their face towards success rather than failure.

When learning to ride a bicycle, a child falls down several times. But does he pay any attention to those falls? No! His eyes are firmly set on riding the bicycle. He wants to see himself cycle stylishly just like the other kids in his neighbourhood. It is this vision of success that quickly propels him towards his goal. But a grownup who doesn't know how to ride a bicycle never wants to give it a try, only because of the fear of falling.

Leaders never cry over spilt milk; they immediately get down to analyzing the causes of failure. They then bury their failures. But before burying, they investigate the failure and seek out all the lessons that can be learnt from it. They use these findings to equip themselves better for the journey ahead.

❖❖❖

Practical Exercise

Offer this prayer now and whenever you need inspiration in the face of failure.

Thank you for making me fearless.

Thank you for making me creative and efficient.

Thank you for work proficiency, writing habit and originality.

Thank you for success in my work.

Thank you for providing everything in abundance.

Thank you for giving me an opportunity to handle responsibility.

Thank you for all the resources.

Thank you for cooperation from all.

Thank you for the feeling of acceptance and fulfilment.

Thank you for appreciation and feeling of brotherhood.

Thank you for self-transformation and self-control.

Thank you for unswerving faith.

Thank you for decisiveness.

Thank you for the desire for social welfare.

Thank you for a virtuous character and resolute intentions.

Thank you for determination, patience, foresight, self-esteem, courage, honesty and holistic growth.

Thank you for endless inspiration and energy.

Thank you for the power of discrimination (viveka).

Thank you for making our mind unshakeable, pure, loving, obedient and integrated.

Thank you for the mantra of complete success.

Thank you for helping us attain the ultimate purpose of success.

What next?

As you overcome failure, it is important to understand how to build courage—one of the most important qualities required to attain success.

22
Cultivating Courage

Courage is an important quality to master in the journey to success. We have come across the topic of conquering fear in the preceding section. We will delve deeper on how to cultivate courage in this chapter.

New activities in your new life are as essential as flowers in a bouquet. Some people find it difficult to start working on new things. When they have a choice between a new, novel task and a routine task, they often find themselves choosing the routine one. They fear that the new task may turn out to be difficult. Apprehensive of entering unknown territory, they do not even make a start. But those who desire self-development take up the new task with courage. If you want to lead a new and successful life, you must experiment with something new every day or at least every week. You must understand well that admission into a new life is gained only by carrying out new actions.

Courage to work with people, to give them feedback and take feedback is also very important. The one who reaches the summit of success does not work alone; many others work together with him which makes it easy for him to reach the peak. The role of the successful person in this endeavour is to gather information about every aspect of the task he has determined to do, and then involve the others in this work.

In addition it is very important to know how the team members feel about doing the work, because negative feelings have an adverse effect on work. The team leaders are the driving force behind completion of work, and it is crucial that they have a positive attitude towards the job. If the leaders have a positive frame of mind, the negative attitude of some other member of the team will not have too much effect. But if the leaders have negative feelings, they must work on changing their feeling, because no work can succeed with a negative attitude.

Taking calculated risks to build courage

Success and courage have a direct correlation with each other. Taking calculated risks is a sign of courage. The question is how to calculate. Here are three steps that shall help you take calculated risks:

1) Ensure that you have the whole information or knowledge that is required to successfully complete the work.

2) Be informed of the percentage of loss you will have to bear in case the venture is unsuccessful.

3) Ensure that you are adequately trained in what you are going to do to accomplish this undertaking.

When you are busy with the new work at hand, some other task may pop up which requires your immediate attention. You should be prepared in advance about how to complete such tasks on time. Often it so happens that if a third task comes to you when you already have two at hand, you show reluctance to do it. You have to be thoroughly trained in handling multiple tasks at a time. This is an
important quality needed for complete success.

Before beginning with any task, plan it down to the finer details so that it becomes easy to accomplish. Include time and space for unexpected urgent tasks too. Thereby any other task that comes up at random will not be a problem to handle. If it does become a hindrance for you, it implies that you have not prepared your plan to perfection. If you are unable to complete your work, it shows that either your plan is deficient or you have a pattern of laziness or procrastination.

When you take up a major project, you have to build your success in stages. For example, if you intend to organize large-scale events in the future, you need training and practice. You need some kind of a platform for training. Small-scale events are like a platform. If you gain expertise in organizing small events, you can back yourself to easily organize larger ones as well. A lot of people will work along with you, and keeping their future in mind, they will learn and understand some things from you to build up their abilities. And you shouldn't run away if you fear that the program would be a failure. Success and failure are two sides of the same coin. Success should not bloat up your ego and neither should failure disrupt your perseverance. You should always continue to develop your abilities.

Think through the activity that you are about to do. What do you want to learn from it? What result do you want from it? When you are clear about this, you will be able to take your next step wisely. Envisage the impact that failure would have on you. If you feel that it will not make much of a difference, then there is no harm in trying new experiments. Don't ever be scared of taking calculated risks.

It is important not to let the feelings of guilt linger in your mind in case you had to abandon your planned program. There is nothing wrong in adjourning a program after appropriate reflection. Focus only on the goal of complete success. Always continue working towards it.

Experiment to increase courage

If you are open and ready to work, you can do any kind of work in any kind of situation and at any time. But take care to ensure that nobody else is harmed when negative incidents occur. If it is not causing any damage to anyone, you can carry out new experiments.

If it is only you who is getting stressed out at work, then there is no harm in experimenting in a new manner. Something negative may occur during the experiment and your mind may comment, 'See! I *knew* this wouldn't work out.' You have to be aware during such moments. You must, as a rule, focus your attention only on the picture of success and not on negative thinking. The mind will keep on running its negative commentary; just ignore it. Try to search for the factors why your tasks could not be done. Also collect more information about that work, so that you will be able to execute such work with ease in the future if it were to ever come your way again. You won't face any difficulty in future assignments if you keep everything pre-planned.

The thought pattern—'I should be successful every single time'—creates the fear of failure. Remember that many a time failure is a part of success. Only after failure can you see those aspects that you had overlooked earlier. Hence never see only one aspect of any incident. Learn to work keeping in mind all the aspects. But always hope for success.

We wish to live in comfort and security. A new activity initially brings a feeling of uneasiness and insecurity, and you do not want that. Hence you avoid any new work. But beginning a new work is another secret of success. Choose the new; the old is what everybody always chooses. The new man of the new age is the one who is successful. He is an inquisitive experimenter, which opens up for him the possibility of the highest development. The fear of failure does not prevent him from taking calculated risks. New possibilities emerge only by taking calculated risks. Courage is aroused by taking calculated risks. Courage increases with experiments. Courage is a sign of success.

Faith in God always gives you courage. Remember that God wants you to succeed and is always there for you.

❖❖❖

Practical Exercise

List down new experiments you are willing to take up in your life. Take calculated risks in your experiments.

What next?

Let us now look at the final realm of success in this book... in the domain of being. Part VI deals with success and spirituality—the hallmark of Complete Success and the beginning of ultimate purpose of success.

Part VI

Success in the realm of being
Uncover the Natural Self within you

23
Self-Experience for Leadership

Every human being performs his deeds and for every deed he desires a reward or fruit. He believes that his work is successful only when his desire for its fruits is met with. But such a desire yields only success, not complete success nor the ultimate purpose of success.

Complete success is attained when you perform your deeds and expect its fruit from the source (God) and not from the channel (man). Complete success is attained when the auspicious desire for the supreme fruit (i.e. *mukti, moksh, nirvana* or liberation) awakens in you. Complete success is attained when your actions (*karma*) originate from your true nature (*dharma*).

Your true nature is formless and limitless. Karma done with knowledge of your true nature no longer remains a duty or a responsibility. It becomes devotion, it becomes Self Expression. These kind of karma are the ultimate purpose of success.

In his ignorance and unconsciousness, man believes success to be the fruit of his efforts. He is disheartened in both cases: when he gets the fruit and when he does not. When he gets the fruit, he considers the person who delivered the fruit to be the source. And, in future, if that person refuses to help him in similar manner, he feels dejected. He considers that person to be the source, when actually he is only a channel. Fruits received from the channel are sometimes sweet and sometimes sour, which make the receiver either happy or sad. There is only one source—God, the Lord, Allah, Supreme Consciousness, Supreme Truth, Self or whatever name you want to give it. Expect your rewards only from Him. Wish for the highest—the supreme fruit—from God, and experience the happiness of attaining the ultimate purpose of complete success. Let this understanding sink in. Understand the actual meaning of success and attain the ultimate purpose of success. This is the whole and sole purpose of human life. When you attain this purpose, you will remain untouched by vices, bad habits and attractions of *maya**, just like a lotus that remains untouched and pure even in swamps.

In the swamp of maya, do you wish to be a lotus in full bloom? Do you wish to attain complete success as well as the ultimate purpose of success? If you do, congratulations! It's your birthday today! Today is your birthday because it is the first day of the rest of your life. It is the first day of your supremely successful life. Happy birthday!

You have been born once; can you be born once again? Yes, you can. The second birth is your real awakening. A bird is first born in the form of an egg. But its real birth takes place when it hatches out of the egg. Man is first born in the illusory material world of maya. And he is born for a second time when he finds out who he actually is, after experiencing the limitless Self (self-realization).

---

*Maya: This whole world including objects, people, time and space is *maya or cosmic illusion.* However, there is a subtle distinction regarding the nature of *maya* versus illusion. Illusion is generally used to refer to something that doesn't exist. *Maya,* on the other hand, is existent and non-existent at the same time, like a dream. The experience you have seems to be absolutely real while the dream is occurring; therefore, the *maya* of this dream cannot be called non-existent. Yet, through the sobriety of wakefulness (self-realization), one can see that the dream was an illusion, a false world.

Do you ever find yourself intrigued by questions such as, 'Who am I? Why am I here? What is the purpose of my life?' Standing in front of the mirror, have you suddenly wondered, 'Who is this?' Or have you ever felt like, 'Is this all a dream? What was it like before the world was born?' If you get any of such questions, there is a reason to it. Not everybody gets such questions. These kind of questions arise in only a few, who then set out in search of the Supreme Truth. In the beginning of their quest, they feel as if they are seeking, but further on they realize that actually they were being sought—by the Truth.

If such questions arise in you too, you need to understand that the answers do not lie merely in words; but in experience. You can know the answers only by experiencing them. Words can be found everywhere; the Vedas, Upanishads and all the holy scriptures are full of words. But the knowledge of words is not true knowledge or wisdom. Wisdom is that which is acquired experientially, which is why it is called as Self Experience. Experience of the Self is an important ingredient of your supreme goal.

❖❖❖

Practical Exercise

If the existential questions like 'Who am I?' or 'Why am I here?' arise in you too, and if you want their answers at the experiential level, you can attend the retreat mentioned on Pg 200 of this book.

What next?

In the next chapter we shall learn how success is your nature.

24
Success is Your Nature

Success is your nature. Progress is a natural phenomenon. Even if man does nothing, nature automatically pushes him towards success. If this is the case, then why don't we see all people successful around us? The reason is that man does not know how to 'do nothing'! Man keeps on doing something or the other out of ignorance and in the process messes up everything. He cannot remain empty in his free time. The very thoughts that he entertains during his free time block his way to success. Thoughts of fear and hatred towards people and various assumptions run through his mind during his spare time. He gets frustrated and subsequently gets into wrong company and adopts wrong methods. This halts the success that was naturally heading his way.

> *A successful farmer always reaps a good harvest because after sowing the seeds, he does not dig up the seeds every day to check how*

much they have germinated. He keeps patience; we need to learn from him. In the spare time that the farmer has at hand, he can learn new techniques of farming. If we too learn how to be patient and free from unnecessary thoughts and how to put spare time to good use, we can surely achieve the aim of Complete Success.

Nature works on its own to cure a sick body. Abundance is the nature of nature. Man could emerge naturally from poverty to prosperity, from gloom to glee—if only his mind could keep quiet. Just when health, wealth and success are about to enter his life, the mind ruins it all with its chatter. The chatter of mind is its thoughts, which actually work like negative prayers. In ignorance, man keeps entertaining negative thoughts, and as a result of these unintended prayers, negative results appear. It is these very thoughts that impede the success approaching you.

There are many instances of people in search of a job committing suicide on the very day that their appointment letter was to reach them. Hence, before your mind turns into a devil's workshop in your free time, fill it with an aim—the aim of complete success.

The pursuit of success or happiness is accomplished by happiness for happiness, by knowing your true nature, your essence. In other words, there is no road to happiness. Happiness is the means as well as the end in itself. Success eludes you so long as you do not realize your true identity. The moment you realize it, success shall be closest to you, or it can be said that you shall be established in the state of complete success.

There is a moment when you are closest to the imminent 'tomorrow' —at 11:59:59 pm. The moment the next second comes to pass, you enter into 'today'. It's the same with success. The moment you come to know your true self, recognize the powers hidden within you, give your thoughts the right direction, and make the most of nature's

boon, you would have entered the realm of success.

◆◆◆

Practical Exercise

List down all the negative thoughts you usually get regarding your goal of success. These are your negative prayers. Now that you are aware of this, drop them immediately and never entertain them in future. Remember success is your nature and you are bound to be supremely successful.

What next?

Success is our nature. If this is the reality, then actually who are we? Let us learn more about it in the following chapter.

25
Become Truthful

Those who want to attain complete success give the highest priority to self-development. Self-development starts from within, which necessitates you to be pure and deceit-free from inside. You have to be true to yourself, you have to tell yourself the truth about yourself. You will have to stay away from deceit. Your inner strength increases when you are free from deceit. And with added inner strength, you can win over any difficulty and become all the more truthful.

Let's go into finer details about the *truth*. The reality is that whatever you have been calling as truth so far is not actually the Truth. You grasp the Truth only when you listen to the messages being sent by life, without making any assumptions. Let's understand this through a small story.

> *After her death, a lady stood at the gates of heaven. Before allowing her in, the keeper*

asked her a few questions. The conversation between the keeper and the lady went as follows:

Keeper: Who are you?

Lady: I am a minister's wife. Allow me in.

Keeper: You are not being asked about your husband. You are being asked about you. Who are you?

Lady: (after a pause) I am an American...

Keeper: You are not being asked about your nationality. Tell about yourself. Who are you?

Lady: (after thinking for a while) I am a mother of three children.

Keeper: You are not being asked about your children. Speak about yourself. Who are you?

Lady: (after a lot of thinking) I am a Christian.

Keeper: The answers you are giving are all wrong. Nothing has been asked about your religion. You are being questioned about you—who you are in reality.

(In this way the lady was repeatedly asked the question and she kept giving the same kind of answers.)

Keeper: Who are you?

Lady: (thinking aloud) Who am I...? Who am I... I... I...?

Keeper: (in a booming voice) Get out! Leave!! As long as your 'I... I...' goes on, you can never know who you really are.

The moment she heard the furious rebuke, the lady sprang awake. It was a dream. But that day, she really woke up. She made a decision to know her real self.

The day we decide to know our real self is the first day of our new life. This is the reason behind the quote: *Morning is when you wake up.* The lady's life changed after that dream. Until that day she believed herself to be the body, mind, wife, mother, and so forth. She was giving all the answers on that basis. But the recognition of her true self proved all her answers wrong. In any other court of law, those answers would indeed be valid. People would say, 'She swore by the *Gita* (or Bible or Koran) and spoke the truth that she is the minister's wife, mother of three children, a Christian, an American...'

Here, we are not talking about the truth as considered by these courts. We are talking about the Truth that transforms lives on listening to it. Listening to whether today is a Thursday or a Sunday will neither lead to self-development nor success. But there is one Bright Truth (*tejgyan*)* which, by mere listening, completely changes your life. It is this Truth that you are being hinted at. The lady in the story considered herself to be the body, which reflected clearly in her answers. But the Truth is something else, becoming Truthful is something else. Being Truthful is knowing your Self and making true progress.

❖❖❖

Practical Exercise

Sit in a relaxed posture and close your eyes. Contemplate on who are you. What are the answers you got and where does it finally lead you?

What next?

Whether the above exercise led you to your true formless self or not, you would have definitely encountered the contrast mind. Let us learn all about it in the next chapter.

---

*Tejgyan: Knowledge of the Ultimate Truth, the Supreme Truth, which is beyond knowledge and ignorance. It is beyond duality and beyond the grasp of the senses. It is the truth about you, about God, about this universe, about life and about so-called death.

26
The Contrast Mind

The biggest obstacle in the way of complete success is our contrast mind.

For the sake of understanding, our mind can be differentiated into two different parts. The first one can be called the simple or instinctive mind. This mind is responsible for the automatic functioning of our body including all the systems (respiratory system, blood circulatory system, nervous system, digestive system, etc.). Also, it is this mind which is at work whenever we are engaged in any activity such as cooking, cleaning, brushing our teeth, driving, writing, painting, accounting—in short any kind of activity. Whenever the simple mind is at work, we are absorbed in the activity at hand and have no other thoughts. That is why the activity is done in the best possible manner.

But as soon as the contrast mind appears, it brings all kinds of disrupting thoughts and spoils the work.

This is the second type of mind. The 'contrast mind' is a term used to signify that aspect of the mind which compares and judges everything. It splits everything into two—white or black (good or bad), just like the contrast control feature in the television or computer. This is the mind that gives rise to fear, worry, envy, insecurity, deceit, assumptions, anger and so forth. It is the root cause of all the miseries in human life. It is present only in humans. It is the one which blocks us from seeing the Truth or knowing our true nature. The contrast mind cannot be moved aside merely with the intellect; understanding of the Truth is essential to do so.

It is the contrast mind that labels everything as either a 'victory' or a 'failure' or either a 'gain' or a 'loss'. This contrast mind is the biggest enemy of complete success. As soon as an incident takes place, it begins its commentary: *'This is good... that is bad... I knew this was going to happen... Now what will happen to me...? Why does it happen only with me...? Why is it always me who has to lose...? Why are people so bad...?'* With its non-stop commentary, the contrast mind hampers all your activities. The only means to topple the contrast mind are: to acquire the right understanding of the Truth, Silence (*moun*), meditation and devotion. This is because right behind the contrast mind lies hidden the nectar of Truth. When the contrast mind falls, the final step towards complete success is taken!

We need to understand the limitations and foolishness of the contrast mind. This is because it's the contrast mind which has wrong thinking and that blocks our progress. Before beginning any work, it first weighs it with its own measuring system and then decides whether to do it or not. If something does not fit into its logic, it comments, 'There's nothing interesting about this task... what's there to be happy about?' We often tend to fall for this comment of the contrast mind. Therefore question your contrast mind: 'Okay, what is the reason you say this? What proof do you wish for? And even if you are shown the proof that there is joy in this task, what will you do? You will take up something else to pick on. Your blabber will continue. This is the real problem.'

The contrast mind is a talking disease; it is a hoard of excuses and comments. There is no need to try to convince it—understand this and you won't be taken in by its opinions and thus be liberated from unhappiness. Unhappiness resulting from the contrast mind's exploits is your real failure.

Know your ignorant mind

When you know that your body has fallen sick and is in a critical condition, your first desire is to quickly get to the hospital and begin with its treatment. Similarly when you become aware of the flaws of your mind, you must take it to the service centre for repair. This is the first step towards success. To become aware of the fact that your mind needs repair (which is possible), is itself a sign of your progress.

Whatever be the kind of body-mind mechanism you have received, if you work on improving it a little every day, you will soon get within viewing distance of the summit of success. The contrast mind will do its best to compare you with others; turn a deaf ear to it. You have no other choice but to work with the body you have received. In fact, if you were to see some of the problems that other people face, you would be staggered. The mind does not pay any attention to what you have; it always dwells on what you don't have. All of these are the habits of the mind that you have to break.

Body — a sealed bottle

A genie was trapped inside a bottle for ages. One day it found freedom from the bottle. You must have read such a story. The bottle here symbolizes our body. Inside the bottle, there is nectar—divine nectar—that is the same in each and every individual in the universe. The bottles may look different—big or small, tall or short, white or black... all have different characteristics and different names. A lot is done to beautify the body and several designations may be given to it, but the purpose of every human body is one: to hold the nectar.

There are bottles all around us, and everyone wants their bottle to go to heaven. Everyone has their own opinion of how this can be achieved. Some politicians advocate that the bottles which break at the border of the country (i.e. soldiers) go to heaven and those which break as terrorists go to hell. Some religions tutor us into believing that those bottles which break for the sake of temples, mosques or churches go straight to heaven and those which fall for addictions go to hell. Are all such beliefs correct? We must understand the purpose of our bottle (body) and taste the nectar (Self, Truth, Everlasting Bliss) hidden within.

> *A man told his friend, 'I saw some goons troubling a weakling. I went straight up to them and gave them a piece of my mind.' The friend asked, 'What happened next?' He replied, 'I don't know what happened but when I next opened my eyes I found myself in a hospital room.'*

Some bottles try to save others, while some try to break others. 'The one who tries to save others goes to heaven and the one who troubles others goes to hell'— such kind of beliefs have been created. Another notion in which a lot of people are caught up is that you cannot get a taste of the nectar present inside you in this lifetime, it is possible only after reaching heaven. A lot of hypotheses about heaven and hell have been postulated. It is okay to begin your spiritual journey based on these hypotheses, but if you remain stuck in this merely relief-providing half-baked knowledge, you will leave this world without knowing the real Truth. And that would be an unsuccessful life indeed.

Contrast mind — the lid

This bottle (body) is sealed with a lid. This lid alone is the obstacle in tasting the nectar. What is this lid and how can it be opened?

The contrast mind is the lid. To remove it, we need an opener. People try various kinds of openers but fail to break open the lid. Various ways to win over the mind are used—chanting, penance, tantra, mantra, karma, dharma—but despite a lifetime of efforts, people do not succeed. So how do we open the lid? Chanting mantras mechanically is of no use. What is needed is understanding. If you get understanding along with the right opener, the lid can come off easily.

Those unaware of the path of understanding suggest: 'Perform *shirshasana* [a yoga posture]. With the bottle kept upside down, the lid will fall off.' Yoga has its own benefits, but it is not useful for unfolding the Truth hidden under the mind.

Each body has a unique constitution. One is hyperactive, another is lethargic and yet another is balanced. Different paths are suitable for different people, but every path must be walked with *understanding*. Several techniques have been propounded to eliminate the mind, but the mind cannot come off without understanding.

Know your body-mind

You can achieve success in the most appropriate manner by knowing your mind and its vices. Everyone's mind has different habits.

> *Two people, who always found it hard to sleep at night, were given this advice: 'When you lie down to sleep, multiply 33 with 27 or some other chosen numbers mentally without using pen and paper. A lot of concentration is required for doing such calculations. After a few such mental exercises, there is full chance of drifting into deep sleep.' The next morning, both of them were asked about their experiment. The first one said, 'Oh, I slept like a baby!' The second one said, 'How could I sleep?! All night I was furiously working with the calculations, scribbling in empty space and mumbling numbers. I couldn't get a minute of sleep and neither could my wife.'*

Understand from this example that everyone has a different body-mind mechanism and each one needs to understand one's own mechanism and accordingly work on it.

Contemplate only on the Truth

The contrast mind has its old habit of thinking about pointless things (the untruth) for hours together. Let your understanding prevail over the contrast mind. Tell it, 'If you want to think about these issues, I give you fifteen minutes a day for this purpose, and no more.' Your contrast mind won't accept it; it will want much more time to think over a problem. But you must obey your understanding. Understanding says, 'Think more about your goal. Think of who you really are and why have you been given this body. Think about the wonders that have manifested in your life. Thus put your body-mind mechanism to proper use.'

Contemplate over the true purpose of your life. You have been given this body-mind mechanism to train it for the ultimate expression of Self. Do not misuse it for the untruth. Let us suppose that your goal is to read a book, which is written in a language that you haven't learnt. So you begin to learn that language. As soon as you have learnt some words, you would immediately want to see if you can read the book. Thus, during your training, you would periodically want to read a few pages of the book to test yourself and judge the level of your progress. When you finally become proficient in that language, you would want to read other books too. But if your contrast mind begins its exploits and misuses your knowledge for worldly gains only, you would be missing the point. If you say that you haven't learnt the language to read the book, what should you be told? You should be reminded that you ought to be doing what you had set out to do. You should understand that the purpose with which you have studied the language needs to be fulfilled first. This is the first priority.

Your body-mind mechanism is a thinking machine. You have received it for thinking and reflecting on the Truth. But you spend your time thinking about everything but the Truth. When you gain conviction about this, you will be able to think that for which you have been gifted this human body.

❖❖❖

Practical Exercise

Contemplate over the true purpose of your life.

What next?

When you contemplate deep enough, there comes a time when all thoughts stop and you reach the state of silence. That is where we are headed in the final chapter.

27
Silence

Moun signifies the state of inner silence which is the intrinsic nature of our true self. It is the state beyond sound and silence, beyond speech and thought. Words appear from this inner silence and also disappear in it. There is silence between every word and behind every word. There is silence between every thought and behind every thought. On the paper of silence, the words of thought are written. To attain this silence is to attain the Self, the God.

This is the Silence we are delving into in this chapter.

> *Once there was a big debate between two friends over: What is the cause of man's suffering and bondage? One of them stated, 'Diseases and physical pains are the cause of man's suffering. If these are eradicated, all his suffering will end once and for all.' The other one said, 'Desires and cravings are the cause of suffering.' The debate raged on but they could*

not settle upon any conclusion. They chewed over this subject from every angle but were unable to find a satisfactory answer. In the end they decided to seek guidance from their Guru.

Their Guru was a Zen master. Zen masters are known to talk less and act more. The two friends presented their case before him. 'We discussed for long about the cause of suffering but could not reach a conclusion. We know that people come to you for acquiring wisdom and achieving liberation from bondage. Hence we request you to resolve this issue. What is the real cause of suffering?' The Guru answered in his own unique way. He thundered, 'Put aside this question and sit down quietly with eyes closed. If you open your eyes, I will pound your head with this cane.' Terrified, the two friends plonked to the floor and shut their eyes without further ado.

They sat there with the thought of being hit on the head running continuously in their minds. When they dared to lift their eyelids a shy bit, they could see the master keeping strict vigil with the thick cane held firmly in his hand. Now they could see the cane even with their eyes closed; so they just sat there quietly without thinking of peeking again.

The master could clearly see the tension on their faces for quite some time, but gradually the tension began to fade.

When you sit in meditation for long, you are initially flooded with thoughts. But when you carry on with meditation despite all those thoughts, you discover many new aspects. People tend to doubt the point of sitting in meditation for a long time. As soon as thoughts begin to inundate them, they think, 'Why don't I get up and do some work instead? My time will be better utilized in finishing some chores rather than trying to find silence which anyway evades me.' Thus most people never sit in meditation for a longer duration. This is the reason that they are unable to become seekers and remain entangled in external things. However, for these two friends, there was no choice. The master was sitting right before them, with a deadly-looking batten in hand. However, the fact is that the master was telling them the answer through this exercise.

A lot of time had passed by and both of them were still sitting in silence. The strain on their faces had eased up. Their thoughts had subsided. The master finally said, 'Now open your eyes, and tell me what is the real cause of suffering?' Both of them answered in unison: 'The real cause of suffering is the mind.'

They had observed that in the beginning when the master had commanded them to sit down quietly and close their eyes, they were flooded with thoughts like: 'Oh dear! Where have we landed up? What's going on? What's going to happen next? How long do we have to sit like this? When are we going to get the answer? When will we go back home? What are the pending tasks at home? Is he going to hit us with the cane?...' When nothing happened for a long time, their thoughts eased up and they felt relaxed.

They felt, 'Maybe our Guru wants to teach us something; he can never intend to harm us.' With this transformation in thoughts, a lot of things began to clear up. The experiment made them see new things.

Often, force is required to attain the Truth. Only upon force does man take action, without which he does not meditate. Let us see what happened next in the story.

After looking at all aspects during meditation, both of them learnt that the root cause of suffering was the mind because they experienced it themselves. Now the debate was over.

Understand from this small but profound story, that if you do not find it difficult to work despite numerous other thoughts, it indicates progress. Sometimes when you begin work, the huge influx of thoughts makes you nervous and it becomes impossible for you to work. But as you go on improving with the art of sitting in silence or *moun*, you realize that all these thoughts can be attended to later, after finishing your work. Right now the work that needs to be done should be done.

If the mind is not disciplined, it gathers a hoard of thoughts in any given situation. It thinks of everything else but the job at hand. If you are able to put off your thoughts for later or give them the right direction with the help of self-suggestions, it is a sign of success. Those who can give their thoughts the right direction always succeed in giving a befitting reply to adversities and make their work successful.

With daily practice of Silence Meditation, you can make the mind your servant and yourself the master. Never allow your mind to interchange roles with you even casually. That is why it is important to practise Silence Meditation every day whenever you get free time. If you don't, your mind will exploit your free time and create unnecessary complications.

There is a big difference in observing silence with understanding and observing silence without understanding. If you are made to sit in silence without the right understanding, your mind will continue spinning thoughts even after you close your eyes. Therefore, when you sit for silence, say to yourself: 'I want a lot of thoughts.' Close your eyes and see what happens. You can do this right now. For two minutes, you have to 'do nothing'. Do not even try to 'not do anything'.

- Sit comfortably in *sukhasana* or *vajrasana* with eyes closed, and watch your thoughts.
- Tell yourself, 'I want a lot of thoughts' and then wait for thoughts. You will be surprised to see that you get very few thoughts.
- Remind yourself intermittently that you want a lot of thoughts, and enjoy the bliss of silence.
- Open your eyes after two minutes.

Do this exercise for two minutes whenever you get free time. Slowly increase this duration. Take it to 20 minutes within a few months.

After performing this exercise, you will find the density of your thoughts decreasing, and you will also learn how 'not to do anything'. Silence will give you the contentment you never experienced before.

People are troubled by thoughts and they wrestle with them to achieve the thoughtless state. You now know that you need not fight your thoughts to become thoughtless. Sit in silence with an intention to know the unseen. Sit for the invisible *nothing*. Otherwise the mind would like to assess, 'What does it mean to do *nothing*? How can I not do anything?' This nothing is altogether different. When the mind falls silent, thoughts stop appearing. The 'nothingness' experienced during that moment is the true *nothingness*. This is what has been referred to as the Bright Nothing, the invisible power, the experience of *samadhi**.

When people observe silence without knowing the invisible power, only thoughts run through them. In spite of being silent for an entire day, they keep mumbling something in their mind. This is not true silence. True Silence is where there are no thoughts, and even if there are, they are watched merely as a witness. Sit in Silence whenever you can remember, even if only for two minutes. If you remember about Silence while watching the television, shut your eyes for two minutes and begin by saying, 'I want a lot of thoughts.' Your thoughts will cease. Your mind may not see its immediate benefits; it may comment that these two minutes were wasted and would have been put to better use by watching the television. But to achieve complete success, you have to make this investment. This investment is a great service unto the invisible (God). You will know this only after achieving complete success at the highest level of consciousness.

Practical Exercise

Perform the 2-minute exercise described in this chapter. Practise it every day while gradually increasing its duration in order to reach the deep state of silence.

What next?

In order to achieve any kind of success, you need to have the intention of achieving it. The power of intention along with daily intentions has been described in the appendices, which can transform your life.

◆◆◆

**Samadhi:* The state of consciousness before time began. Samadhi is a state which cannot be adequately described in words; it can only be experienced. It can be said that samadhi is being conscious of the true Self, transcending time and space. Or being in the state of undifferentiated beingness; a state of complete calm, tranquillity and joy but where the mind continues to be alert.

Appendices

Power of Intention

Consistency is the key to success.
Consistent practice leads to complete development.
When all your possibilities are realized through consistent practice,
complete development is achieved.

Self-discipline is an eessential ingredient of complete success. Self-discipline can be cultivated in your body by taking up one intention per day and fulfilling it conclusively. If you are able to honour your intention, you are well on the road to complete success.

In the olden days it was a custom to offer flowers before the idol of God. Every morning when one placed a flower before God, one would take an intention for the day. The offering was meant as an oath to abide by the intention. Two flowers offered to God would mean that two intentions were taken up for the day. This custom served to increase one's awareness about this oath and made sure that one successfully followed it all day long. The purpose behind this tradition was to increase will-power, because it is will-power that brings any work to fruition.

When man takes up an intention/resolution before God, it makes him committed to it. He cannot breach a promise made to God. The custom of offering flowers was created for this purpose. A small flower can go a long way in your growth. By working on one intention a day, you can summon your powers of discipline and self-confidence. This confidence becomes the causative factor for complete success.

After you work on 30 different intentions for one month, restart the same cycle next month. On the first day of the next month, you will not have the same experience that you had on the first day of the current month. In your first attempt at that particular intention, you may not have remembered it even once throughout the day. In the evening you may have felt dejected at your failure. But remember, this is an experiment which requires perseverance. Just take the dejection in your stride and begin the next day with fresh resolve and intention of success. Give it your best shot and seize every opportunity you get to implement your resolution. Don't take a single day off from this experiment. This is a very important exercise for self-development. You can either work on one intention per day or one per week, as per your convenience.

A list of intentions has been provided below. Experiment with them as they are, or add a few more of your own. Remember that the purpose of these intentions is to practise for self-development. The success of each experiment is a step towards achieving the ultimate purpose of success.

◆ ◆ ◆

Daily Intentions

DAY 1

Carry out every action today with complete awareness and viveka.

This intention is essential for raising the level of your awareness as well as your consciousness. You carry out many actions in a state of unconsciousness, due to which your mind wanders into the past and future. This intention will help break this habit of the mind and teach you to stay in the present. This new habit of being in the present will slowly but surely pervade your entire life and fill it with awareness. Awareness will bring in wisdom and you will live a balanced and equanimous life.

Today you must do the tiniest of things with complete awareness—brushing your teeth, washing utensils, wiping the table, wearing shoes, scratching your head, walking, sitting... everything. Keep an eye on all your activities while you get up, walk, sit, read, write, etc. At your workplace too, carry out every action with awareness. Be on the watch: Are you banging things on the table without awareness? Are you speaking on the phone unnecessarily? To observe and understand these things, you need to be alert. And to be alert, you need to do everything with awareness and viveka.

This resolution of today will help awaken your awareness and viveka. With awareness and viveka, nobody can smoke a cigarette, utter an abuse or do anything bad. All unnecessary things happen only in unconsciousness. Once you are on the alert, everything will take care of itself and you will automatically do the right things. This step you take today will prove to be a foundation for complete meditation and complete success.

DAY 2

Today or for the entire week, do not talk anything unnecessary or undesired.

Today you have to abstain from speaking excessively. Be less verbose in your talk; use as few words as possible to get your message across. Do use your common sense, though, while attempting to fulfil this resolution. If you use too few a word and people find it difficult to comprehend you, then you obviously need to use more words. But your effort should be to cut out the unnecessary words.

Throughout the day, one utters a lot of words which are not required at all. These redundant words eat up your time and energy. Thus, save your time and energy and savour silence. This practice will help you to start getting rid of everything unnecessary in your life.

DAY 3

Do not hurt anybody today through your words or actions.

As per today's intention, you have to abstain from undesirable words that can hurt others. Bitter words also create cracks in your relationships. The disposition of 'not speaking anything undesirable' saves you and others a lot of time and energy. After today's experiment, you will want to continue it further. After you have worked on each one of the resolutions, you can take this one up again. Eventually this will turn into a good habit. It is habits that build your character. And only the strength of a fortified character pulls success towards you.

When you try to acquire all the required qualities at one go, you will fail in this attempt. However, when you choose them one at a time and carry out a few experiments by awakening the power of intention, you achieve success in your every attempt very easily and become a master of all virtues.

Man is a social animal. He needs support and guidance from people to live and succeed. If he hurts people with his words or actions, he creates obstacles for himself. Out of hardened habits, he unwittingly hurts others and then defends himself by saying, 'I only said the truth.' But you can always convey the truth in a polite manner that doesn't hurt people's feelings. You can talk in a soft, pleasant tone too.

If your actions and feelings hurt others very often, work seriously on this intention today. Your feelings are not immediately recognized by people, but words and actions are. Take care of them.

This intention is a spiritual practice to mend your behaviour. Everyone needs to learn this practice and control his words and actions for giving a love-filled response to every individual and situation.

DAY 4

Today save as much money as possible and spend wisely when required.

Alway carry this understanding with you regarding wealth: Allow wealth to enter your home but not your head. And never ever let it enter your heart. Sit in your car but do not misconceive that you are the car. Rise above your car in spite of being inside it. If you are not able to do this, the car is useless for you.

Money is a path, not the destination. But the path must be a firm one. If the path is full of pits and mounds, the destination seems to be far away. Those who save money save themselves from many a worry of the future. If you pay a little attention to how you spend money, you can save a lot of it. Else, you will never know in your unconsciousness when your entire wealth is finished. The fondness of saving money is very dear to Goddess Laxmi (the Goddess of Wealth). The money you save will act as a magnet for bringing you more money. Thus, with this small intention of today, you can open up great possibilities.

Nobody can become rich by earning huge sums of money if he spends all that he earns. You become rich by acquiring the understanding about money. The keenness to save money is the first rung in the ladder to prosperity.

Today, whenever you are about to spend money, ask yourself whether it is your 'need' or 'want'. When you are about to buy something from the market, ask yourself: 'Is buying this item my need or want?' If your needs have been fulfilled, you can buy that item to satisfy your want. But, in general, buy things according to your needs, and you will not face money problems.

People buy things only because their neighbours or colleagues have them. They do not really need those things, but they are just so influenced by others that they end up buying things that they are never going to use. As per today's intention, you shall spend your money wisely. You shall buy only what you need. What decides whether a man is rich or poor? It depends on the answers to these questions: Is he able to save money? Does he spend his money wisely? Does he utilize his wealth to help him walk the path of Truth? The truly wealthy possess the wealth of health, love and virtues. You too can become one; today's resolution will help you in this effort.

DAY 5

Today complete every task that you have decided to do.

This intention is the most potent weapon to strengthen your will-power. It combines the two qualities of decision-making and completion. The art of decision-making is something that everybody needs to learn as soon as possible. You will become an expert in decision-making only after you practise this art with small, day-to-day decisions. With consistent practice, you will achieve a level that people will marvel at. They will be amazed by the accuracy and swiftness of your decisions, when earlier you could not even select clothes for yourself. When you work on today's intention, you will eventually be able to take bigger and better decisions with ease. It will instil in you a great deal of self-confidence.

Every one must adhere to this intention until one's body gets disciplined. There are innumerable jobs left incomplete in the world as of date. Only completed jobs enhance the beauty, worthiness and possibility of our planet. If you have done thousands of tasks but none of them are complete, the result is: *failure*. A 'jack of all trades but master of none' is always a failure. With today's intention, decide to undertake minor tasks and make sure you complete them. The self-confidence gained thus will prepare you for your greatest self-expression, hence work on this intention with all the dedication you can muster.

It is possible that you make some wrong decisions in the beginning, but this will only teach you the nuances of decision-making. Hence start with small decisions today and make them happen. You can definitely do this much today. Finish all your decided tasks before going to bed tonight.

All the right decisions you take will create a bright future for you, and conversely all the wrong decisions you take will lead you to an unhappy life. Always, therefore, use your power of viveka to make decisions. Using viveka is to use your intellect and heart in balance.

The decision to stop taking decisions due to the fear of making wrong decisions is a wrong decision. Successful people will tell you that the secret of success is 'to not fear making wrong decisions'. You have to learn how to turn wrong decisions to your advantage. This is how you will gradually learn to make right decisions. Practise taking decisions using your viveka all through today. Decide and do it; it will prove to be a right decision. Do what you are afraid of doing. If you are afraid of making decisions, start with small ones and take it from there. Very soon you are going to like this day.

DAY 6

Express your gratitude to God today.

As soon as you wake up today, offer your gratitude to God. Say, 'Dear God, thank you for a good night's sleep. Thank you for showing me a bright new day. I shall spend this day with joy and make good use of my time. I shall lift the level of consciousness of every person I come across today.'

This intention of today is a golden opportunity to look back at all the good things, virtues and blessings that God has bestowed upon us. This intention evokes love and devotion towards our Creator. Those who know the power of devotion repeat this intention every month. As you contemplate you will slowly recognize all the grace and blessings you have been showered with.

When you pray, you ask for a lot of things from God. But when you reflect on all that God has already given you unconditionally, your prayer reduces to just one word—'Thanks!' When you get this understanding, you would be thankful even for this 'thanks'. Your life itself will become gratitude.

When you pray to God with this feeling of gratitude, God bestows you even more freely because that feeling makes you all the more receptive. God always wants to give; it's only us who do not know how to receive. If someone sits with an umbrella over his head and says 'I want sunshine', how can he receive it? Unless he removes the umbrella, he's not going to be touched by the sunlight. Therefore, remove your umbrella of ignorance by expressing gratitude to God, and pray to Him, 'I need sunshine, bless me with the shower of thy grace.' It's not that you should thank God only after you receive something, but you should learn to thank Him even before you receive it. In fact this will ensure that you definitely receive it.

DAY 7

Today pray for one and all.

Pray not just for yourself but for everybody today. Let everyone benefit from your well wishes and prayers. In turn you will benefit a thousand-fold. This is the amazing and generous law of nature.

Your presence should be such that your mere presence benefits everyone around. Even if you do not utter a single word or carry out any activity or help anyone, people should still be able to gain by your presence. This can happen only when your heart is full of compassion, love and prayer. Hence pray to God for the progress of everyone: 'Dear

God, grant everyone with all that they need for growth—whether health, wealth, love or virtues.' Always harbour feelings of well-being and success for all.

DAY 8

Do not criticize anybody today; only speak well about everyone.

Criticizing others makes the mind feel good; it wants to do it again and again. When you work on today's intention, this wrong habit of your mind will start breaking and soon your mind will become pure, loving, obedient and unshakeable.

On the other hand, when someone criticizes you, just remember what Saint Tukaram has said: 'It is good to have critics as your neighbours.' He said so because if the person criticizing you is right, then you will correct yourself, and if he is wrong, you get a chance for spiritual practice. Either way, it is you who gains. But do not conclude from Saint Tukaram's words that you have to be a critic for others, because by doing so you will only harm yourself and cultivate a bad habit. As a critic, you will only find flaws in others; you will never notice their virtues.

As soon as you see a negative habit in someone, you feel like telling that person that he is wrong. But today you have taken an intention of not criticizing anybody at all. You may certainly tell him about his mistake tomorrow if you wish to, but not today. Thus if you do want to offer your criticism, do it tomorrow and do it in a better way than your ingrained tendency. Learn how to 'criti-guide' others, i.e. offer constructive criticism in a positive manner intended to provide guidance rather than pointing out faults. Free yourself from the habit of criticizing. This will earn you cooperation from others and improve your relations.

If you want to censure or ridicule someone only because you feel an itch to do so, it is of no good to anybody. But if you wish to see an improvement in someone, it is fine; yet do not try to achieve this today through criticizing. Today's intention is to stay away from criticism and to speak well about everybody. Appreciate the good qualities you see in people. You probably admire someone's handwriting, someone's voice, someone's punctuality... let them know that you have noticed these qualities in them. Tell them whenever you get a chance to. Take up this resolution with a special intention of following it today so that you develop a habit of seeing virtues in everybody, be it your servant, your wife, your children, neighbours, friends or any other acquaintances.

DAY 9

Put everything in its right place today.

There should be a place for everything and everything should be in its place. This intention of today is like a protective shield for your time. People tend to misplace things, and when those things are needed, they waste valuable time looking for them, not to mention the anxiety and irritation. Consequently they are unable to finish important tasks and may even incur monetary loss. By embracing this good habit of keeping things in place, you will prepare yourself for a bright future.

At the outset, you may not appreciate the significance of this intention, but it can actually help you in all areas of life—physical, mental, financial, social and spiritual. The habit of keeping everthing in the right place will not just help you to keep external things in order, but also the things inside your brain. That includes what you hear, read, etc. Are you able to keep these internal things in order? Can you remember and recall them in a systematic manner? Are you able to remember names of people easily? When you store something in your brain, it should pop up as soon as it is required to. If you do not store information in the right place, you cannot find it when you need it. This is the biggest problem of students who fail in examinations. Therefore, be it objects or information, you must cultivate the habit of putting them in their appropriate and allocated places. The external intention will automatically help you to bring about internal order.

When you practise upon this small intention for a few months, it will prove to be beneficial not just for you but for your family members a well. They will find things exactly at the place they should be, without a moment of delay.

DAY 10

Work on your health today. Do not eat unhealthy or excessive food.

Most people hardly pay attention to their health in today's busy world. Following this intention once every month, you will develop a respect for your health. Better your health, better is your world. Stand in front of the mirror and challenge yourself: 'If you have guts, get fit and prove yourself.'

With this intention today, read books on health and add to your knowledge about health. Follow a different diet today. Speak to health-conscious people and create a new set of rules for you to follow. Dispose off the medicines from your closet that have expired. Spring-clean both your body and your house. Recollect the things that you have forgotten about health. Write down all the information you may have collected on health matters.

Exercise and health are closely related. Often people think about exercise only after falling sick. You should develop the habit of regular exercise while you are still healthy. It's easy if you take a solemn oath to do so. Gradually you will see that you will get into the habit. If not daily, you can start exercising two or three times a week and build it from there. Reading health literature will motivate you. You might also want to work on your breathing. Whenever you remember to, take a long, deep breath. Think to yourself, *'With every deep breath, I am inhaling good health and releasing all toxins and diseases from my body. I am developing great health so that I can easily express myself at the highest level.'* You can express yourself at the highest level only if your body supports you. Hence make exercise a compulsory activity in your routine. Single out the parts of your body that need special attention. Check by bending in different directions whether you experience any pain. This will indicate which parts need exercise. If you consciously exercise one day, you will realize its importance. Be sure to dig your well before you are thirsty.

'As is the food, so is the mind. As is the mind, so is the world.' We become what we eat. Therefore take a look at your diet. Does your diet induce laziness? Does your diet induce restlessness? Your diet must be balanced and holistic.

The food you eat not for appeasing hunger but to satisfy your taste buds and greed is totally undesirable. Excessive food harms you, but you make up some excuse and allow yourself to binge. Even if you eat healthy food excessively, it is as good as eating unhealthy food. Anything in extreme is harmful. Decide today that you shall always tread the middle path and never eat unhealthy or excessive food. Eat only as much as the body requires.

With this intention you will take the first step towards good health. It is food that brings you either good health or bad health. If you are able to exercise control over your tongue for one day, then one can expect you to achieve the highest goal too.

DAY 11

Read or listen to something on spirituality and self-development today.

Readers are leaders. The habit of reading endows you with the wealth of information and knowledge. When you have all the information, you can take all the correct decisions. And only the correct decisions lead you to success. If you want success, you certainly need to take up the intention of reading. Choose the right books to read. The book in your hand right now is a right selection you have made. Such books help you to develop yourself. Books on spirituality and self-development awaken faith towards life. And in faith lies the seed of complete success.

Spirituality is not something distinct from life. It is the actual spirit of life. Life itself is spirituality. If you contemplate a little on spirituality, or pick up a line said by great saints and ponder over it, a miracle can indeed occur in your life. The purpose of making you read or listen to spirituality is to have you contemplate over it profoundly and to implement it. Only contemplation makes you implement it, and implementation brings about a transformation in life. Your old life is merely a repetition of your tendencies, whereas a transformed life is the ultimate purpose of complete success.

Some books make for a superficial read, some provoke deep thought, and some are bought to cherish and read for a lifetime. Always select the right books. If you practise the little, simple steps given in these priceless books, your life will be blessed with health, wealth, Truth, fulfilment and success.

DAY 12

Do not watch television today.

Do not watch television for entertainment today. Watch only educational or informative programs, or if possible, avoid watching it altogether. However, if you insist that watching some particular program is essential because you gain something from it, then you may watch it. But do give this experiment a try today. Do not park yourself in front of the television. If you are compelled by habit, do one thing—sit on that couch, but with the television off.

What do you think of cheap friends who eat away your time? Don't you tend to avoid them? If you do, why do you stick to the television? TV is the biggest time-eating friend you have today, and cable TV is its tail. People get entangled in this tail and waste precious time. At this point you may want to put forth the good qualities of this friend, but today we are not discussing about those. This friend of yours dupes you by showing a few good things.

Hence maintain a distance from this television and watch only pre-decided programs. This will save you ample time which you can utilize for reading enlightening books or rendering service.

Do you feel that it is too difficult to avoid the television? If you do, today's intention will benefit you the most. Firmly resolve that you will not watch it, at least for today. The most difficult of things are accomplished by starting with baby steps. By skipping the telly for one day, you might well get a chastening experience that will awaken a new thinking, understanding and awareness in you.

DAY 13

Today, do everything on time and in less time. Strike a balance between work and rest. Do not do anything in haste.

Time is invisible but powerful. Even a little work done on time is useful, while any amount of work done after the time has gone by is useless. Plan your work in keeping with time, else you will find your work incomplete at the end of the stipulated period. If you want to make the maximum of the invaluable time you have at your disposal, today's intention will always be of great help.

Today's intention is most useful for lazybones. Lazy people have the habit of cooking up one excuse after another to put off today's work to tomorrow. You have to be alert to finish your work in less time, as today's intention is to work as efficiently as possible. Those who are slow at work need to work on increasing their pace.

How to do the work that you have been doing for months and years in a better manner and in less time? The answer to this question is in today's intention. Work on it and you may well see a miracle happening in your life. You will keep getting better and better, day by day.

People waking up on time in the morning not only save themselves from the hassles and irritations of rush hour, but also reach their offices well on time and avoid the needless troubles, running, screaming and stress. People who complete their jobs as per their commitments do not feel the load of the next job beforehand. They are ever ready to take on every job that they need to do. Some people get disconcerted when a new job arrives before the earlier one is over. The commitment to begin and end a job on time always keeps you ahead of time and free from the bondage of time.

Practise time management techniques today. Before retiring for the night, go over the next day's program in your mind. Think about the hurdles you are likely to face and the solutions to overcome them. When you do this, you will actually see that the next day goes as planned and you will be able to keep your word. Develop mastery over the principle of achieving more using less time and effort.

For those of you who are the restless type and cannot sit in one place for long, your intention today is that you will not do anything in haste. As such, you must never do anything in haste, but pay special attention to this today. Complete all your tasks one by one with a calm mind to get the right outcome. Anything done in a hurried and disorderly manner is shabby. And once you get habituated to such a work culture, it will influence all other areas of your life. None of your tasks will ever be done well. If you try to work on all your tasks together, it's going to worsen the situation. Hence this intention is crucial. Today's intention is sure to develop physical discipline in both types of people—the lethargic and the hyperactive.

Apart from that, maintain a balance between work and rest today. Balancing work and rest means resting before you get tired and working before you feel lazy. If you take a little rest when you get a hint of tiredness, you will be able to do more work subsequently. Similarly, you must start working before you feel lazy, else you will just waste away the day sleeping, and when you finally manage to get up in the evening, you will still not feel like working. Such rest is useless. Striking a balance between work and rest is an art that you must acquire. It will act as a tonic to gain expertise and remain ever so youthful.

DAY 14

Do not harbour feelings or thoughts of hatred and aversion in your mind today.

The hearts of those who forgive remain clean. Often the cause of heart attack is either hate attack or head attack (thoughts of malice and revenge). Learn the art of forgiving yourself as well as others, and let the feeling of love radiate from your heart. If at all the power of feelings can be misused, it is by harbouring hatred and cruelty in mind. If you have the feeling of revenge, it will harm you first. Today, replace such feelings with those of love.

At the beginning of the day, make a list of the people you hate, either slightly or strongly. Then, whenever you get some time during the day, bring them up one by one before your mind, talk to them and forgive them. You often think more of the people you strongly hate. When you forgive them, you too are liberated from the clutches of hatred. By forgiving others, you are not doing them a favour; it is a favour you do upon yourself. At bedtime, pray for all those people you had loved to hate. The power of prayer will free you from hatred. You can offer the following prayer:

> *'Dear God, please bless these people with your grace*
> *and fulfil their desires according to the divine plan*
> *you have designed for them.*
> *Remove all the blockages inside them,*
> *so that they can live their life happily*
> *and let others live happily.*
> *I forgive all of them, whom you have already forgiven.*
> *Please give me the strength to forgive.*
> *Thank you.*
> *Amen.'*

DAY 15

Talk to everyone in a polite, soft and sweet voice today.

Your tongue can either place you in the cool shade or incinerate you in the blazing sun. This two-inch long tongue can make wonderful new friends for you or deposit you in hell. The resolution of working on your speech can solve plenty of your problems.

The tongue is flexible and the teeth hard. Teeth can break in old age but the tongue continues to run sharply like a pair of scissors. This flexibility of the tongue is like a blessing, due to which it remains safe in the midst of hard teeth. Work on today's intention so that this blessing does not turn into a curse.

Being flexible, the tongue slips very easily. In the flow of talk, if someone pronounces a word wrongly due to slip of tongue, he feels embarrassed. But the same person feels no embarrassment when abusive words, sarcasm, curse or lies emerge from his tongue. Those people who resolve to use their tongue carefully always stay happy.

Remember that wounds inflicted by sticks and stones heal sooner or later, but wounds inflicted by words may fester for a lifetime. Keeping this in mind, carry out today's intention with all your heart.

In addition you have to specifically keep your voice soft. Whenever you speak to somebody, ask yourself whether you can say the same thing in a soft voice. Do apply common sense though. You cannot call out to someone standing far away from you in a soft voice and expect him to respond appropriately. Thus speak softly today, but using common sense. You will feel so good when you speak softly that you would want to continue with it every day.

DAY 16

Today respect everything—living or non-living.

The feeling of love is the highest feeling. In love, you respect not just living beings but also seemingly lifeless objects. For example, when you are in the experience of love, you will shut the door gently instead of banging it. Today's experiment will be of great help in awakening the feeling of love within you. In the beginning you may not feel anything towards lifeless objects. But persist with this experiment because you have resolved to. As you go on doing it on this day of every month, you will soon experience the feeling of oneness. Even if you do not experience that feeling, this day will teach you a lot. You will feel increased awareness towards things. You will look at even little objects with deeper attention. We pay attention to things we respect. By doing so, you will also acquire the art of observation. The power of observation will benefit you in various ways in future, but remember that you are not doing this just for its benefits. Your aim is to awaken and enhance the feeling of love and respect.

Living beings like dogs, cats, crows, parrots, pigeons, cows, bulls, etc. are all around you. Develop a new understanding towards them. You have seen these animals before, but today look at them as if you are seeing them for the first time. Look at the life inside these animals. It will teach you something about life. The right perspective will surely evoke unconditional love in you.

DAY 17

Contemplate over the mistakes you made during all the incidents that occurred today and what you learnt from them. Accept every incident that took place.

Why is man unhappy? The cause of his unhappiness is the contrast mind. What is it that the contrast mind does that creates unhappiness? The contrast mind weighs between the good and bad, and rejects the bad part. Unacceptance creates misery. Acceptance is happiness, while unacceptance is sorrow.

Today you have to know this secret experientially. Accept anything and everything that happens today, whatever it may be. Also note down what happens upon accepting some situation. When does it become easy to accept something and when does it become difficult? Keep note. After having seen all the games that the mind plays, you will become more mature. You will be astonished on experiencing the power of acceptance. As soon as you accept something, both of your hands become free to tackle the situation. You can then easily find the solution to the problem. When you do not accept the situation, you suffer, you are unable to solve the problem, and you also spread unhappiness among those around you. Therefore try this experiment today and watch how the magic of acceptance works in your life.

Day-to-day matters that make you unhappy due to unacceptance can be: the newspaper delivery boy coming late, running out of hot water for your bath, household help not turning up for the day, your dress getting burnt by an overheated iron, your watch getting misplaced, broken slipper or shoe, running out of gas, hike in gas prices, not reaching the station on time, your shirt getting soiled, not being appreciated in spite of doing a good job, unable to get a ticket at the movie theatre, a grudging shopkeeper, fruits turning out to be sour, death of a person who had borrowed your money...! Accept all such situations and move on. You will experience instant relief when you do so.

When you face any of such situations, explicitly ask yourself the question: 'Can I accept this?' Surprisingly, your answer will be a 'yes' almost every time. God has given man enough strength to accept any situation. Man can endure everything from the scorching heat of the Sahara to the biting cold of the Himalayas. To appreciate the whole beauty of the power of acceptance, you can read the book *Secret of Happiness*.

DAY 18

Stay away from assumptions today.

To make assumptions is to form an opinion about something without having adequate information about it, just like shooting an arrow in the dark. On doing this repeatedly, you become habituated to presuming things. This can only lead to more suffering and in fact becomes an additional cause of suffering. If you are already sad, this habit doubles your sorrow.

Look at every incident with a new perspective, without assuming anything. Very often you form opinions about people just by looking at their appearance. *'This man looks like a villain from a movie; he must be bad.'* The reality may be far from it. The writer of a movie has no option but to cast faces as demanded by the film's characters; and we start judging people we come across on that basis. Good people are found in any disguise.

Most of the assumptions made by an individual turn out to be wrong, and yet he does not give up this habit. Based on every word that someone speaks to him, he assumes and concludes that the person must have said that with so-and-so purpose in mind. 'He wants to put me down; he wants to hog all the credit...' But later when he meets up with that person and speaks his mind, he realizes that what he was thinking had no trace of truth in it, and that the real reason was something else, about which he had no idea at all. Often we make a mountain out of a molehill.

Judgments made with complete information are not assumptions, but experience. Assumptions made with incomplete information are nothing but games played by the mind. The day you abide by the intention of not making any kind of assumptions, you will learn plenty.

When you watch a movie, if you don't make any guesses, you enjoy it till the end. If you make guesses, you mostly get bored and leave the movie hall. Likewise, do not spoil the fun of this movie of life with your presumptions and speculations. Watch the drama of your life unfold, without getting stuck to any scene. Very often you are able to see things happening with others without making any assumptions, but not with yourself. Hence work on this intention at the earliest in order to cut short the string of assumptions.

DAY 19

Stay away from dishonesty in all situations today.

Today's intention is to stay away from dishonesty. Deceit and cunningness are habits of the mind stemming from fear and greed. Man tends to hide certain things from others due to insecurity. He lies when asked and beats around the bush when he speaks about those things. While speaking of others' virtues he moderates the facts, but while speaking about himself he overstates the facts.

Many a time people mislead others with wrong information out of greed for gains. They don't hesitate to deceive others to make some extra bucks. This habit worsens into an inexorable disease. Then they start deceiving themselves too. They hide their own truths from themselves. Their progress stops at all levels. Those who can arouse their power of intention never block their own progress. Today, take the first step towards a completely honest life.

Talk to yourself honestly today. Tell yourself your truth: 'When do I deliberately obstruct others in their work? When do I happily work for someone? What are the jobs that I do only because of fear? What are the jobs that I take up due to greed? What are the things I do for the sake of boosting my ego? What are the things that hurt me and make me feel bad?'

Today, take an intention of refraining from the smallest of lies, even if you feel it's harmless. For example, do not reply to the concerned person that you have finished a job when you haven't. You may be just about to do it, and that person would never come to know whether you had done it then or sometime later. So, you may feel like 'what's the harm in saying that I've already done it?' But it is these little things that slowly develop into a hardened habit of lying. Hence today refrain from the smallest of lies.

At the least you must never be dishonest to yourself and your doctor. In case you have back pain and you tell the doctor that you have abdominal pain, who is going to suffer? You. The doctor will treat you for the ailment you complain of. Understand from this example that only by telling the truth, you will be able to overcome every hurdle and achieve true success. Tell yourself the truth about all the vices and flaws you have that need to be eradicated. Do this today.

DAY 20

Donate to the right place today.

When you give, the feeling is that of love, but an action-oriented one. The feeling of faith gives us reassurance, and faith in action makes us fearless in our activities. In the same way, donating is love in action. Donating is not confined to money as most of us think. A donation can be in several forms—manual help, blood donation, participation in a social cause, etc. Even if you give someone your time or some useful suggestions, it is an act of donation. Today's intention is to donate wherever you see a need.

Whatever you give comes back to you multiplied several times, if you give with a feeling of love and the right understanding. The capacity to give varies from person to person. Give as much as is possible for you. Do not donate out of a feeling of compulsion or duty. Donate to the right place with a feeling of goodness in your heart. When you do this, your donation becomes a seed that shows your faith. Do you have faith in the law of nature that whatever you give comes back to you? It is your faith that converts your seed of donation into a 'seed of faith'. Sow a seed of faith today. To understand more about the seed of faith, you can read the book *Excuse Me God*.

Be careful not to feed your ego while donating. It should give rise to happiness. 'I am giving because God has given me' —always harbour this feeling of grace in your heart.

DAY 21

Train your hands today.

When you see a juggler in a circus juggling several balls at a time, you are left amazed by his dexterity. You wonder how he can do it with such ease. But understand that when he was practising his art, he was not on stage. That period of time is not visible to you. It takes the juggler several years of rigorous practice before he reaches the pinnacle of success. Though you do not have to join the circus, there are some things in life for which you need to train your hands, ears and eyes.

You have to work on improving the ability of your hands through exercise and discipline. People should be pleased to shake hands with you. Your hands should be steady and should perform the right actions. Listening to Truth discourses is training for your ears and looking at the good in others is training for your eyes. As long as you have ears, eyes and hands, you will hear, see and do things. But what should your ears listen to? What should your eyes look at? What should your hands do? This decision is to be made by you, with discrimination and firm resolve.

Also see to it today that you don't do anything carelessly. Do not leave anything half-done. Do everything in a proper manner.

DAY 22

Train your ears today.

Let your ears be the channel that lead you to walk on the path of Truth and attain the ultimate purpose of your life. Unless someone tells you the ultimate purpose and unless you listen to it, you cannot work on this mission. If somebody is constantly drawing your attention towards your ultimate purpose, let your ears be open for it. Shut out the places where you hear mockery, abuses, bad things or negative news. Affirm to yourself and to the universe that you want to hear only that which is good and that which is the Truth. Trust it when you hear something good—about people, about things, about the world. Resolve to listen to only good people who will take you on the right path. Go for a spiritual discourse today. This is training for your ears. Let your ears become tuned to receive the highest truth and divine guidance. This will pave the way for your ultimate success and happiness.

DAY 23

Train your eyes today.

Let your eyes see only what you want to see. Do not focus on things you don't want in your life. See only those things that enhance your equanimity and inspire you to tread the path of Truth. If you see the wrong kind of things, you will see the same in your dreams. Not only will you have troubled sleep, you will also spoil your day. Hence train your eyes to see only the Truth.

You may have observed that when you misuse your eyes and watch movies showing horror, violence or obscenity, those scenes keep playing before your eyes throughout the day. It is okay if this happens once in a while, but if you get habituated to watching such kind of things, you will seriously damage your life. Without any hesitation or delay, start training your eyes before you form a wrong habit.

Your hands, ears and eyes should do nothing without your permission. Once trained, no wrong scenes or words can enter you. Words and scenes have a deep impact on you. They keep running in the subconscious mind. At the slightest opportunity, they manifest either in your dreams or in reality. Be very alert about what you hear and see.

Thus, cut out the unnecessary, see the goodness around you, observe the good deeds being performed by people, and appreciate the beautiful scenes of nature. This is your intention for today, which will prove to be very helpful.

DAY 24

Contemplate today on what you have lost and what you have gained in life so far.

Man is the only animal in the world which can think and contemplate. It is contemplation that has led him to scientific inventions. Only through contemplation has he been able to give himself direction. Without direction, man's life is worse than that of an animal.

Today is for reflecting on all that you have gained and lost in life so far. How important were the things you have lost? How useful are the things you have gained? If what you have lost was very important and what you have gained is not useful, it indicates that you have been living an unconscious life.

Some of the good things you may have lost due to bad habits could be friendship, positive thoughts, creative ideas, good advices from someone, etc. Somebody may have been asking you to attend a spiritual retreat and you may have been avoiding it. You could be repenting your decisions now, since you now know that if you had implemented those advices and teachings in your life, your life could have been different.

This reflection will bring you to a new understanding for your future life. At the least it will ensure that you do not repeat the mistakes you have been making so far. A new life will await you, in which positive, creative and constructive work will happen through you.

Today is your chance to meditate on every aspect of your life, thus ensuring that you have the best times ahead. If you do not retrospect today, you will keep getting the same that you have got so far. If you want a new and brighter future, do work on today's intention.

Those who contemplate deeply discover the subtlest and finest secrets of life. And this enables them to usher in a revolutionary change in society. Today will be the day you sow the seed of a reformation. Imbue your mind with the intention of establishing peace in the world through contemplation.

You can also think about how you can perform your routine activities today in innovative ways.

DAY 25

Observe today the virtues in others and imbibe them into your life.

Observe only the virtues in whoever you meet today. Whatever you focus on automatically gets assimilated in you. Good qualities will come into you when you keep your attention on them. Hence, keeping this intention in mind, contemplate on the good qualities of anyone you come across.

This is also the secret behind idol worship. When you sit before an idol of God and worship, you actually ponder over the qualities of the Divine. For example, the big ears of Lord Ganesha remind you to learn the art of listening and to increase your listening power.

If you reflect on divine virtues, very soon you will see them developing within you. People do not know this principle and spend an entire lifetime performing meaningless rituals in the name of worship. In that process they cannot imbibe any divine virtue. Today's intention will teach you to enhance your qualities by observing them in others.

DAY 26

Meet new people today.

As per today's intention, you must meet new people today. It will help you to become more social and also enhance your self-confidence. When you talk to them, you will discover that people are not as bad as you had imagined. Don't go by their appearance; people are indeed nice. Also, remember to focus on their good qualities. This experiment will bring forth new possibilities for you. Use this experiment to learn the art of human relations.

DAY 27

Today, constantly be in the present.

Almost all the time, man is lost in the thoughts of the past and future, whereas only the present is the Truth. The past is dead. The future is only in our imagination. The Truth is—the present. The present moment is the Truth, and we have to learn the art of living in this moment.

If at all you need to go into the past, it should be only to learn from your mistakes. Become a Superman and take a quick little trip into the past. And when you need to plan for a future activity, become a Spiderman! Throw your web exactly in the direction of your goal, quickly swing into the future and sketch your plans for a brilliantly executed job. This is all you have to do. You don't have to stay long in the past, nor in the future. When you stay in the Truth of the present, you will achieve real success.

DAY 28

Today, while constantly living in the present, smile for no reason throughout the day.

You have to live in the present as well as smile even without any reason today. Smiling throughout the day is possible. You need to acquire certain understanding for that. But for today, whatever be the level of your understanding, recollect that wisdom repeatedly and smile. You laugh a lot at others, but today smile at yourself. Observe your antics through the day and smile. Watch how you talk to people, how you exaggerate or understate the facts, how your behaviour changes when your boss is around, how you behave with shopkeepers, how you treat the maids at home, and so on. When you watch yourself in all these situations, you are sure to laugh at yourself. You will realize and smile at your own double standards.

The habit of smiling without reason and smiling at yourself awakens a positive feeling within you. By observing your activities, you will not only understand your nature, you will also feel happy inside.

In addition, this experiment will help you to develop a good habit of smiling, which will improve your interpersonal relations as well as win you the cooperation you need from others.

The bigger the success you aim for, the greater is the support you need from people. You have seen how people form human pyramids during the festival of *Krishna Janmashtami*. Higher the clay pot containing the prize, more is the number of people required to work in unison. A smile helps you to work in a team. Try out this experiment today.

DAY 29

Be happy throughout the day today, no matter what.

Happiness is not just the destination of every human being, it is also the way. Thus, if you want to attain happiness, take an oath to be happy today in every situation—good or bad. With this experiment, you may be surprised to discover that only because we don't harbour a firm intention to be happy or we don't try to be consciously happy, we feel neutral or unhappy most of the times. Always being miserable is a habit, so is always being happy. You can cultivate this habit. You can always be happy. Whether you believe it or not—this is a fact. This is because nobody and nothing can make you unhappy, unless you allow it to. So, do you want to allow anybody to make you miserable? It's your choice. Besides, your intrinsic nature is happiness. You are happiness. Hence it is possible. Once you have fulfilled this intention successfully for one day, you can try it the second day and the third. If you can do it for 108 days, happiness will become your nature. (It already is; just let it surface.)

DAY 30

Today, do not use the words 'I', 'me' and 'mine'.

Take an intention for today that you will not use the words 'I', 'me' and 'mine'. You will often feel the need to use these words while communicating with others. For example, 'I have to leave now; I will be completing this work tomorrow', etc. But before you do, take a pause and think whether you can say the same thing differently. If somebody asks you, 'Who kept this jug of water over here?' Before you answer 'I did', pause. Think of how you can say the same thing without using the word 'I'. You can laughingly say, 'Guess who?' He will say, 'Oh, so it's you who kept it here.' You can say, 'Yes, who else?' In this way, staying alert you will speak in a different manner because you cannot use the word 'I'. This will in turn awaken your awareness.

You use the words 'I', 'me' and 'mine' to address yourself. Although they help make conversation easier, their usage creates an illusion. When you say, 'I went to the market', you refer to your body as 'I'. When you say, 'I imagined' or 'I thought', you refer to your intellect as 'I'. When you say, 'I am sad' or 'I am bored', you refer to your mind as 'I'; because the body can never be sad or bored.

Now give this a thought. If you use the word 'I' to refer to three different things, then who is the real 'I'? Sometimes you say, 'I am a Hindu, I am a Muslim, I am a Gujarati, I am a man, I am black, I am intelligent...' and sometimes you say, 'I am a teacher, I am a brother, I am a husband, I am a mother...' In this crowd of thoughts, the real 'I' is lost. That is why you are being asked to take this particular intention today. If you cannot totally avoid using the word 'I', at least reduce its usage to the minimum possible for you.

After having worked on the resolution of not using 'I', 'me' and 'mine', comes the next step—that of knowing the real 'I'. The definition of the real 'I' varies in every person's life. However, the real 'I' is who you actually are—not the body, not the mind and not the intellect. You are the one beyond all these. The mere existence of who you are has created this whole world. To know this real 'I' at the experiential level, you can participate in the Magic of Awakening Retreat.

Who am I? Where am I? Why am I here? What is enlightenment or *moksh*? Is it possible to attain *moksh* in this lifetime? If you have such questions, this retreat is the answer. Let the Magic of Awakening Retreat be among your top priorities as it offers you a stress-free and fearless life, liberates you from sorrow as well as the one who feels sorrow, dissolves all your problems at once, frees you from negative thoughts and leads you to self-realization, thus granting you with an easy, straight, powerful and prosperous life.

This retreat has been attended by thousands of seekers and is a must for every Truth lover to increase his wealth of consciousness and achieve complete success. On being blessed with divine wisdom, you will not be the same person as you are today. You will leave the path of false happiness and begin to tread the path of true happiness and achieve the ultimate purpose of success. Further details of this retreat are provided on the following page.

◆◆◆

You can mail your opinion or feedback on this book to:
books.feedback@tejgyan.org

About Sirshree

Sirshree's spiritual quest, which began during his childhood, led him on a journey through various schools of philosophy and meditation practices. He studied a wide range of literature on mind science and spirituality. After a long period of deep contemplation on the truth of life, his quest culminated in attaining the ultimate truth.

Sirshree espouses, "All spiritual paths that lead to the truth begin differently but culminate at the same point – Understanding. This understanding is complete in itself. Listening to this understanding is enough to attain the Truth." Over the last two decades, he has dedicated his life to raise mass consciousness.

Sirshree has delivered more than 4000 discourses that throw light on this understanding. He has designed a system for wisdom, which makes it accessible to all. This system has inspired people from all walks of life to progress on their journey of the Truth. Thousands of seekers join in a virtual prayer for World Peace and Global Healing daily at 9:09 am and 9:09 pm.

About Tej Gyan Foundation

Tej Gyan Foundation is a non-profit organization founded on the teachings of Sirshree. The Foundation disseminates Tejgyan – the wisdom that guides one from self-development to Self-realization, leading towards Self-stabilization.

The Foundation's system for imparting wisdom has been assessed by international quality auditors and accredited with the ISO 9001:2015 certification. This wisdom has been presented in a simple, systematic, and practically applicable form that makes it accessible to people from all walks of life, regardless of religion, caste, social strata, country, or belief system.

The Foundation has centers in more than 400 cities and towns across India and other countries. The mission of Tej Gyan Foundation is to create a highly evolved society by leading seekers from negative thoughts to positive thoughts and further, from positive thoughts to Happy thoughts. A 'Happy thought' is the auspicious thought of being free from all thoughts, leading to the state of supreme bliss beyond thoughts.

If you seek such wisdom that leads you beyond mere knowledge, dissolves all problems, frees you from all limiting beliefs, reveals the true nature of divinity, and establishes you in the ultimate truth, then it is time to discover Tejgyan; it is time to rise above the mundane knowledge of words and experience Tejgyan!

The MahaAasmani Magic of Awakening Retreat

Self-development to Self-realization towards Self-stabilization

Do you wish to experience unconditional happiness that is not dependent on any reason? Happiness that is permanent and only increases with time? Do you wish to experience love, peace, self-belief, harmony in relationships, prosperity, and true contentment? Do you wish to progress in all facets of your life, viz. physical, mental, social, financial, and spiritual?

If you seek answers to these questions and are thirsty for the ultimate truth, then you are welcome to participate in the MahaAasmani Magic of Awakening retreat organized by Tej Gyan Foundation. This is the Foundation's flagship retreat based on the teachings of Sirshree.

The purpose of this retreat

The purpose of this retreat is that every human being should:

- Discover the answer to "Who am I" and "Why am I?" through direct experience and be established in ultimate bliss.

- Learn the art of living in the present, free from the burden of the past and the anxiety of the future.

- Acquire practical tools to help quieten the chattering mind and dissolve problems.

- Discover missing links in the practices of Meditation (*Dhyana*), Action (*Karma*), Wisdom (*Gyana*), and Devotion (*Bhakti*).

About Books by Sirshree

Sirshree's published work includes more than 150 book titles, some of which have been translated into more than 10 languages. His literature provides a profound reading on various topics of practical living and unravels the missing links in karma, wisdom, devotion, meditation, and consciousness.

His books have been published by leading publishing houses like Penguin, Hay House, Bloomsbury, Wisdom Tree, Jaico, etc. "The Source" book series, authored by Sirshree, has sold over 10 million copies. Various luminaries and celebrities like His Holiness the Dalai Lama, publishers Mr. Reid Tracy, Ms. Tami Simon and Yoga Master Dr. B. K. S. Iyengar have released Sirshree's books and lauded his work.

The Source
Attain Both, Inner Peace and Worldly success

Awaken the Power of Faith
Discover the 7 Principles of the Highest Power of the Universe

To order books authored by Sirshree, login to:
www.gethappythoughts.org
For further details, call: +91 9011013210

SELECT BOOKS AUTHORED BY SIRSHREE

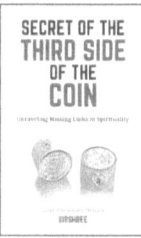   

To order these and other books authored by Sirshree
Visit **www.gethappythoughts.org**

Tej Gyan Foundation – Contact details

Registered Office:
Happy Thoughts Building, Vikrant Complex, Near Tapovan Mandir, Pimpri, Pune 411017, INDIA. Contact: +91 20-27411240, +91 20-27412576

MaNaN Ashram:
Survey No. 43, Sanas Nagar, Nandoshi Gaon, Kirkatwadi Phata, Off Sinhagad Road, Taluka Haveli, Pune district - 411024, INDIA. Contact: +91 992100 8060.

WORLD PEACE PRAYER

Divine Light of Love, Bliss, and Peace is Showering;
The Golden Light of Higher Consciousness is Rising;
All negativity on Earth is Dissolving;
Everyone is in Peace and Blissfully Shining;
O God, Gratitude for Everything!

Members of Tej Gyan Foundation have been offering this impersonal mass prayer for many years. Those who are happy can offer this prayer. Those feeling low or suffering from illness can receive healing with this prayer.

If you are feeling troubled or sick, please sit to receive the healing effect of this prayer. Visualize that the divine white healing light is being showered on earth through the prayers of thousands and is also reaching you, bringing you peace and good health. You can dwell in this feeling for some time and then offer your gratitude to those offering the prayer.

A Humble Appeal
More than a million peace lovers pray for World Peace and Global Healing every morning and evening at 9:09. Also, a prayer (in Hindi) to elevate consciousness is webcast every day on YouTube at 3:30 pm and 9:00 pm IST. Please participate in this noble endeavor.

www.ingramcontent.com/pod-product-compliance
Lightning Source LLC
LaVergne TN
LVHW040145080526
838202LV00042B/3025